THE COMPLEAT SMUGGLER

THE ATTACK ON POOLE CUSTOMS HOUSE

The Compleat Smuggler

A Book about Smuggling
in England, America and Elsewhere
Past and Present

by

JEFFERSON FARJEON

ILLUSTRATED

THE BOBBS-MERRILL COMPANY
Publishers

INDIANAPOLIS   NEW YORK

FIRST EDITION

PRESS OF
BRAUNWORTH & CO., INC.
BUILDERS OF BOOKS
BRIDGEPORT, CONN.

Printing Statement:

Due to the very old age and scarcity of this book,
many of the pages may be hard to read due to the
blurring of the original text, possible missing pages,
missing text and other issues beyond our control.

Because this is such an important and rare work, we
believe it is best to reproduce this book regardless of
its original condition.

Thank you for your understanding.

CONTENTS

Contents

>>>>>>>>>>>>>>>><<<<<<<<<<<<<<<<

LIST OF ILLUSTRATIONS

FOREWORD

I SHALL not bore the reader with a long preface. He will probably consider this volume quite long enough without it. But it is, to me, a novelty to write a book which has not depended wholly, or almost wholly, on my own imagination or experience, and I find myself left with a sense of gratitude to those without whose labor this present labor of mine could not have been completed. I want to acknowledge the assistance I have had both from writers who are alive and from others who are dead, and to record my thanks to them.

My firsthand knowledge of smuggling is negligible. I have never participated in its performance or its prevention. To the little I have known and seen, I have added the much that I have read and been told, and I have tried to weave it all together in a form that would give old matter new life. I have also tried to make this a volume that could be dipped into by the reader with ten minutes to spare, or perused from beginning to end by the reader with ten hours, plus an indomitable courage! Whether I have succeeded, the future will show. At the moment of writing these words only one person has enjoyed this book—namely, myself—and even for that singular enjoyment I must award the credit to the subject.

Indeed, smuggling is such a fascinating subject—so much more fascinating than I realized before I began delving into it—that if I have produced an uninteresting volume on the theme I shall at any rate have accomplished a unique achievement!

My title, of course, is sheer bluff. To write a "compleat" history of smuggling would require a dozen volumes of this size; and then indeed I might cheat my own object by wearying my reader instead of entertaining him. But did Isaak Walton say all that was to be said about angling? I am quite willing to stand in the dock with such a distinguished fellow prisoner.

And now, to conclude where I began, let me name some of the works, and some of the writers, to whom I owe my gratitude. To the list below should be added encyclopedias, dictionaries of dates, official records, local guide-books, and many lists and statistics.

SMUGGLING DAYS AND SMUGGLING WAYS, by H. N. Shore; SMUGGLERS AND SMUGGLING, by A. Hyatt Verrill; SECRET HIDING PLACES, by Granville Squiers; THE SMUG-GLERS, by Lord Teignmouth and Charles G. Harper; HISTORY OF THE MURDERS OF WILLIAM GALLEY AND DANIEL CHATER, by "A Gentleman of Chichester"; RUM, ROMANCE AND REBELLION, by Charles William Taussig; CONFESSIONS OF A RUM RUNNER, by James Barbican; SMUGGLERS OF TODAY, by W. J. Makin; THE VOY-

AGE OF THE "DAYSPRING," by A. C. G. Hastings; JEAN
LAFITTE, by Mitchell V. Charnley; HANGING IN CHAINS,
by Harkhorne; AUTOBIOGRAPHY OF A CORNISH SMUGGLER,
by Henry Carter; THE KING'S CUSTOMS, by Acton and
Holland; SMUGGLING IN THE SOLWAY, by J. Maxwell
Wood; MEMOIRS OF A SMUGGLER, by Jack Rattenbury;
FOOTPRINTS OF FORMER MEN IN FAR CORNWALL, by the
Rev. R. S. Hawker; HISTORY OF GUERNSEY, by Jonathan
Duncan; TALES OF AN OLD SEA PORT, by W. H. Munro;
MARGARET CATCHPOLE, by the Rev. Richard Cobbold;
LOUIS MANDRIN, by F. Funck-Brentano; ECONOMIC AND
SOCIAL HISTORY OF NEW ENGLAND, by W. B. Weeden;
etc.

To all who have been named, and to some who
have not, my thanks.

J. J. F.

Introducing the Smuggler

SMUGGLING is a crime with many advocates. Those who defend it do so, frequently, for the sake of their own consciences, just as they make a virtue of cheating the railway or the income tax. But the smugglers of the good old days were on the whole a sad and sorry lot, and some of the crimes they committed would, if described in detail, make the most hardened thrill-writer wipe his forehead. Those details will be lacking in these pages. There is quite enough without them.

Nevertheless, the justification which smugglers so persistently, and at times so ingeniously, claimed for themselves cannot be set aside when one considers their

13

case; and, ethically viewed, they stand considerably higher than the pirate and the highwayman. When in fact they drifted, as they not infrequently did, into the practice of direct thieving on land or sea, even in their own eyes they fell very definitely from grace.

The pirate and the highwayman had no motive beyond their own personal profit. No principle was involved, and they richly deserved the gibbet when they came to it. The smuggler, on the other hand, was generally pitting his courage and his wits against laws which to his intelligence had every appearance of being genuinely unjust, and which very frequently were. While it may be assumed that the average smuggler was inspired by the prospect of making a bit and would not have risked freedom and life merely to defend the right, he did reduce the cost of living for—literally—millions of poor people for whom prevailing prices were exorbitantly high. This was not only his justification but his support.

Quite half of England sided with him, giving him both sympathy and assistance; otherwise he could never have prospered as he did, or become such a distracting problem to riding officers, revenue cutters, coast guards, and sorely harassed governments.

There can be no doubt about it, smugglers as a class were popular.

We are indebted to the writings of the late Rev. R. S. Hawker, of Morwenstowe, Cornwall, for some interesting opinions expressed by smugglers and those in sympathy with them. The worthy clergyman did his best, against rather heavy odds, to spread the legal as well as the Christian ideal in his locality. He tells us that one lawbreaker, possessing a financial interest in spirits—not the kind of spirits Mr. Hawker himself was interested in—failed utterly to understand why a king should tax good liquor. Taxes, conceivably, were necessary. But why *liquor?* Why not something else?

If Mr. Hawker had had the time, he could have responded by reeling off over a thousand other articles that were being similarly badly treated!

Another unrepentant member of his flock took him to task for urging the view that it was not quite cricket to kill officers of His Majesty's revenue who were performing their duty, however unpalatable that duty might seem to the "gentlemen." This was the dignified term the smugglers chose for themselves.

"There have been divers parsons in my time in this parish," the smuggler fan exclaimed admonishingly, "and very larned clargy they were, and some very strict, and some would preach one doctrine and some another, and there was one that had very mean notions about running goods, and said 'twas a wrong thing to do—but even he and the rest never took no part with the excisemen!"

The argument being, apparently, that to object to an exciseman's death was to show undue partiality.

In spite of this, the average smuggler did not kill for fun—quite often, indeed, he ran away to avoid being killed himself—and he generally realized that the excisemen were honest if misguided people. He preferred them dishonest, and frequently made them so by bribes and promises. Then he had nothing whatever against them. He never extended any leniency, however, to that most hated of all individuals, the informer, and no crime seemed more contemptible to him than that of spying on his activities. And this in spite of the fact that he had to do considerable spying himself.

To be an informer in those days—an informer was a person who passed on to customs officials information deliberately or accidentally acquired—was to take your life in your hands. Without some compelling motive such as a stern belief in assisting the law, a hatred of smugglers as a class or of some smuggler in particular, or the prospect of blood money, nobody would undertake the risk. The terrible retribution that had befallen many informers deterred all but the bravest or the most avaricious from chancing a similar fate. Even to be suspected of informing was enough to bring danger to one's door, for criminals do not offer their victims the fair hearing they themselves receive, and suspicious smugglers were often ready to deal summarily with suspects in the complete absence of any real evidence.

Here is one case. It is one of the cases that shall be told briefly, shorn of its horrible details. A gang of smugglers had concealed some bags of tea in a barn at Yapton, near Chichester. When they went to collect the bags, they found them gone. Suspicion which appears to have been wholly unjust fell upon a poor laborer.

A couple of the roughest members of the gang—their names were Mills and Curtis, the latter being a butcher in more senses than one—visited the laborer and found him threshing corn. Without telling him their business they invited him into the road, put him on a horse, and conveyed him to an inn on Slindon Common, the Dog and Partridge, where the rest of the gang were waiting. Here, in a back parlor, the terrified laborer was put through it. There was no proof whatever that he had either stolen the tea or informed the excisemen of its whereabouts, and he swore he knew nothing about the matter. He was stripped and subjected to the most appalling tortures. The poor fellow did not leave the inn alive.

Such cases were the exception rather than the rule, but there was no exception to the rule that informers,

whether maltreated or not, were the outcasts of smuggling society.

The Rev. R. S. Hawker gives one more illuminating glimpse of the contempt in which these civilian spies were held, and after the above grim story we turn to the genial Cornish clergyman with some relief. If we can eliminate from our minds the sinister background, we will find humor in the following account.

Mr. Hawker is writing of an aged predecessor at Morwenstowe.

> While this venerable gentleman was presiding at a parish feast, in cassock and bands, and presented with his white hairs and venerable countenance quite an apostolic aspect and mien, on a sudden a busy whisper among the farmers at the lower end of the table attracted his notice, interspersed as it was with sundry glances towards himself.
>
> At last, one bolder than the rest addressed him, and said that they had a great wish to ask his reverence a question, if he would kindly grant them a reply; it was on a religious subject that they had dispute, they said. The bland old man assured them of his readiness to yield them any information or answer in his power. "But what was the point in dispute?"
>
> "Why, sir, we wish to be informed if there were not sins which God Almighty would never forgive?"
>
> Surprised and somewhat shocked, he told them "that he trusted there were no transgressions,

common to themselves, but if repented of and ab-
jured they might clearly hope to be forgiven."
But with a natural curiosity, he inquired what
kind of iniquities they had discussed as too vile
to look for a pardon.

"Why, sir," replied their spokesman, "we
thought that if a man should find out where run
goods were deposited, and should inform the
gauger, that such a villain was too bad for mercy!"

Morwenstowe was not the only village in which
clergymen found themselves in embarrassing situations. In every county from Cornwall to Kent, and
round the corner up the east coast to Norfolk, they
were given hard nuts to crack, and they were always
liable to receive particularly awkward examples of the
trust and understanding they themselves preached.
After landing a cargo of run goods, the smugglers'
next step, unless conditions were exceptionally favorable, was to conceal the contraband till it could be
conveyed to its final haven for disposal. Caves, farmhouses, barns, inns—some inns were entirely run by
smugglers—lofts, cellars; these and other repositories
were used or adapted for their part in the great game
of cheating the excisemen.

But the game did not always go as planned. An
informer may have been too busy, or a watcher too
smart. Then an emergency hiding place had to be
found till the weather cleared, and who could be better trusted in man's extremity than a servant of God?

Thus it befell one memorable day that a country
parson, showing his bishop over his church and angling for approval, suddenly came upon a corner of
the stone floor piled high with cases of brandy and
tea. The bishop, of course, was himself an understanding man!

Another parson received a similar shock in different circumstances. He walked to his church to conduct a service, and to deliver a sermon which would
help his congregation to believe in the goodness of
life, and incidentally of himself. When he reached the
church he was informed somewhat excitedly that the
service would have to be canceled.

"Why?" he inquired.

The convincing answer came, "The pulpit be's full
o' tea and the vestry wi' brandy!"

Situations like these had to be accepted in those
truly amazing times, and they were usually accepted
with grace. As compensation for the shocks they imposed, the owners of the tempting casks and cases,
when they duly performed the nocturnal removal job,
always left one behind. This, even to parsons, improved the complexion of things.

In those days, as now, politics had great power to
confuse men's moral sense and create situations in
which, deserting the true instincts that companion
simple thinking, one easily juggled black into white.
If the smugglers were bad, bad laws helped to make
them so.

The smugglers so far referred to were products of

the eighteenth and nineteenth centuries; but long before these arose to cheapen prices by their own particular methods, poor people had suffered beneath unjust legislation. There do not seem to have been any
serious revolts against Ethelred for imposing the
Billingsgate toll of a penny on sailboats and a halfpenny
on smaller boats. Later injustices, however—the customs of "purveyance," "prisage," and "butlerage"—
caused the populace to express their discontent in
words and deeds. The various devices for raising
money were for the King's personal aggrandizement
or pleasure, and being bled by a bad individual is
even more irritating than being bled by a bad government.

There were two methods by which reigning monarchs enriched themselves, or sought to meet their
creditors, that made the people particularly bitter, and
they are quoted here to show that the smugglers of a
later date had good precedents for their belief that,
under certain provocation, it is justifiable to take the
law into one's own hands.

By the first method the King claimed goods from
merchants as payment for their privilege of conducting
legitimate trade. The people paid for these goods by
the inflated prices charged by the merchants to cover
themselves. If the King wanted more goods than he
normally received, but doubted whether he could
claim more without meeting protests, he purchased
the commodities at a price fixed by himself—a low
price of course—and sold his surplus at a high price.

As he saw to it that he had a surplus, he became a sort of smuggling merchant himself—though, in his royal case, authorized.

By the second method, instituted when the profits from the first ceased to cover his elaborate expenses (and there was no one in those days to limit his expenses), he borrowed money from the rich foreign merchants, generally, Italian, and granted them the farming of the customs. In effect, he pawned this source of the country's revenue.

Very naturally, the English poor had no love for the foreign merchant, and there were often lively scenes at the ports and along the trade routes. If an Englishman cracked a foreigner's skull he committed a legal and moral offense, but his temptation was as sore as the foreigner's head.

Yes, the smugglers undoubtedly had their precedents for objecting to impositions that resulted in high prices. It is doubtful, however, whether they ever combed history for their justification!

A smuggler is a wretch who, in defiance of the laws, imports or exports goods without payment of the customs.

DR. JOHNSON

I like a smuggler; he is the only honest thief.

CHARLES LAMB

Baa, Baa, Black Sheep!

THE connection between sheep and owls may seem obscure, but owls work by night, and so did the original wool-smugglers. For this simple reason the wool-smugglers were called "owlers." They were also called "caterpillars," which from a certain angle was far less appropriate. The human caterpillar acquired a nimbleness of movement quite unknown to the insect.

Owlers were not the pioneers of smuggling. The Phoenicians had a word for it, and the smuggling history of Carthage should make picturesque and lurid reading. If smuggling is not as old as man—the embargo on fruit in the Garden of Eden was spiritual, not legal—it is as old as money and the first laws to maintain money's unequal distribution.

The wool-smugglers of Romney Marsh, however, who rebelled against authority in the thirteenth century, were literally the forerunners of the first great smuggling movement in England, a movement which was kept up for over five hundred years till it merged into the smuggling proper, or improper, of more recent times.

Wool-smuggling was an inversion of the more familiar process. The wool was not smuggled into the country but out of it. And for this reason.

The wool-growers, being the humblest members of the woollen industry, were fleeced no less than their sheep. On the other hand the weavers, being more well-to-do, had to have their interests preserved, and this was achieved by closing the door to foreign competition and forbidding any wool to go out of the country.

This was, of course, a cruel blow to the sheep farmers. Their fine-quality wool was a staple item in Flanders. With this market closed down, surplus stock accumulated, and the English weavers could use the situation to force down prices.

The English weavers, in fact, won both ways, because they not only bought their wool cheap, but did not have to compete in the home market against foreigners whose weaving was far superior to their own. It is difficult to understand why the English weavers were inferior in their work. Theirs was not a new industry in the country. The Romans, during their occupation of Britain, established a woollen factory at Winchester, and before that, Queen Boadicea is described as wearing "a tunic checked with a variety of colours," which is supposed to have been a woollen garment manufactured by her own people. By the thirteenth century they might have been as skilled in cloth-making as any.

The results of this injustice, perpetrated with a strange lack of vision, were soon apparent. They were, in the condition and temper of the country, inevitable. Governments have created many strange situations, but this one was particularly Gilbertian, and it was obvious that if the English weavers could not demand as much wool as the farmers could supply, while across a small strip of water the demand was endless, something would have to be done about it.

The sheep farmers found their solution in the owlers.

It was fortunate that those portions of England nearest to the Continent were best adapted to the owlers' purpose. Romney Marsh was a perfect spot for their operations, and the intricate waterways of Kent and Sussex became alive with secret, nocturnal traders. If the farmers did not know how to handle boats themselves, they found plenty of others who did in counties famed for seamanship, and the organization grew quietly and expanded mightily.

While the owls hunted food in the forests, the owlers hunted the wherewithal for food in hidden storehouses, small boats, dark winding streams that flowed toward the sea, and on the sea itself.

The penalty for a slip leading to detection was death.

As the owlers, by their illicit methods, improved
the condition of the sheep farmers, the weavers who
had profited by their trials became glum, and they
looked toward the government to readjust the situation once more in their favor. The owlers being too
nippy to be caught, further legislation was needed.
The obliging government did its best to find a brain
wave.

The brain wave was found in 1276. Subtle in its
intention, it was almost pathetic in its futility. The
ban against the exportation of wool was removed, and
in its stead a tax was imposed with the object of making the now-permitted exportation unprofitable. The
export duty was threepence a pound. The full value
of wool at that time being eighteenpence a pound, this
duty deprived the wool-grower of a sixth.

But necessity had caused the owlers to discover
their power. Drive any people to distraction, and, unless you stamp them out, they will blunder into a solution that will make the distraction boomerang back.
The solution of the owlers was perfectly simple.

"Why should we pay this threepence?" they asked,
conscious of their success. "They can't catch us! Let
us go on as before!"

So they went on as before.

And so did the government. That is to say, the
government went on being stupid, as before. Incred-
ibly stupid, surely, even for a government? After
twenty-two years of failure, the export tax of threepence was increased to sixpence—from one-sixth to

one-third of the full value of the wool. This, of course, merely augmented the incentive to continue the smuggling. The new threepenn'orth of tax did not make one ha'p'orth of difference.

This Battle of the Wool became an epic. It raged with varying fortunes for over another four hundred years. The owlers became as much a part of national life as were the American freebooters during Prohibition, but they did not have it all their own way. Lean times came, and toward the end of the fourteenth century many farmers had large stocks of wool on their hands with no hope of selling it. Lest the golden goose should die, England was forced to allow general export again. The golden goose began to recover. Immediately squeezing by taxation recommenced. The owlers renewed their efforts and once more saved the situation.

And so it went on, law and lawlessness following each other around in a vicious circle.

It seems incredible that, after first discovering the words "owler" and "caterpillar" in our history, we may turn four hundred years of pages and still come across them. We find Charles II pondering over the problem of the smugglers, reintroducing the total ban on the export of raw wool, and reviving the death penalty for the crime. In order to propitiate the cloth merchants, Charles II instituted a new law which was as remarkable as it was unique. He decreed that every man should be buried in a woollen shroud. This amazing law actually remained in force from 1678 till

1815, though whether it was scrupulously kept all that time is another matter.

In the next reign we find a story * which illustrates the might of the owlers, and is typical of many others. It deserves its space.

The hero, or victim, of this incident was one William Carter, excise officer for King James II in the Romney Marshes. A man with a stouter heart or a shrewder brain would have seemed a better selection for this particular district, for Romney was owler land and fairly creeping with caterpillars. Devilish ticklish country, from the exciseman's point of view.

Still, William began well. Acting upon accurate information, he surprised a gang of owlers on the road between Folkestone and New Romney just as they were about to run wool across the Channel in French boats. This time the boats did not sail. William and his men bagged nearly a dozen scamps and took them in triumph to Romney.

Then he interviewed the Mayor, and, presenting his papers, requested that the men should be lodged in prison pending their trial.

To his astonishment, the Mayor refused his request. William was either very ignorant or very simple. All the Mayor would do was to release the owlers on bail, and the bail he fixed was fantastically light. The Mayor had two very good reasons for his disappointing attitude. One was his fear of the owlers; he understood the district, if William did not, and he was not

---

* For details of this narrative the author is indebted to A. Hyatt Verrill's *Smugglers and Smuggling.*

going to risk having his skull broken. The other was that he hoped to retire one day with a sound bank balance as well as a sound head. His investments, if they had a name, were Owler Enterprises.

But the Mayor bore William no ill will for having interfered with one of the enterprises. He gave him some fatherly advice, and suggested that the excise officer leave Romney as quickly as he could.

William accepted the advice. So did his crestfallen men. Developing the fastest speed consistent with what remained of dignity—the dignity was less than the speed—they reached the town of Lydd in surprisingly good time, and tumbled into an inn to rest.

Here they received another disappointment. The alarmed innkeeper did not want them to rest. William insisted, however, and regretted it that night. The owlers, now augmented to fifty, and armed with weapons of about fifty different kinds, made a night attack upon the inn in order to teach the Law a lesson. William waited anxious for the light. It was long in coming, for the month was December. When it came, astonished to find himself still alive, he managed somehow or other to escape with his men, and they raced for Rye.

The inflamed mob followed. The excisemen had no dignity at all left now, so pace could develop without a brake. Perhaps it would be kinder not to visualize the Law clambering up creek-banks, floundering through marshes, and sticking in mud. But, after all, this particular story is comedy, not tragedy, and a grim end was averted by the discovery of two or three convenient boats at Camber Point. William and his breathless men fell into them, and just had the time and strength to push off before their pursuers arrived.

The Carter incident was surely one of many. The owlers carried on with impunity, until William of Orange took the matter in hand and, by instituting new laws, tried to succeed where others had failed. One of the most interesting of his devices, and that possessing the most amusing sequel, was a fifteen-miles limit. By forbidding anybody to buy wool within fifteen miles of the coasts of Sussex and Kent, and imposing the severest penalties on defaulters, he hoped to keep the wool in the country; but the effect was merely to give the wool-growers and the owlers a little more trouble, which they willingly undertook. They went inland till the coast was fifteen miles away, transacted their business there, and ultimately disposed of the wool in the usual manner!

Foolish laws were not the only reason for the failure of authority. There were not enough officers to see that the laws, foolish or otherwise, were carried out, nor were the officers paid sufficient to insure their enthusiasm. One has only to consider the difficulty of their job, and the small remuneration it carried, to understand how easily they fell to the temptation of bribes. When in due course the dragoons came along to assist them, it was hoped that an improvement would set in, but once more hope was disappointed. The dragoons, worse paid than the riding officers, were still more open to corruption.

Wool-smuggling continued for another hundred years, but its greatest days were now over; the cause of this was not the law, but alternative attractions. Wool languished, from the smuggling point of view, as liquor, tobacco, tea and countless other forms of contraband arose. Gradually the ever-growing smuggling fraternity began bringing things into the country instead of sending them out, rejoicing in the golden opportunities afforded by Protection. Another factor which hit the owler was that his Continental customers were becoming wise and breeding their own sheep.

Well, the owlers had had a long inning. If they scored slowly toward the end, the score mounted to five hundred years before circumstances bowled them out, and their name and their activities slid back into history. Only their ghosts live now in the marshes and dykes and creeks; and if you meet one, he will doubtless say:

"Don't you go thinkin' 'twas the law what beat us! 'Twas liquor and 'baccy and tea, and suchlike. Times ain't what they was. You can't beat wool!"

From a proclamation issued on August 9, 1661:

"A sort of leud people called Smuckellors,
never heard of before the late disordered times,
who make it their trade . . . to steal and defraud
His Majesty and His Customs."

A-Smuggling We Will Go

H O W was it that smuggling, unlike other crimes
that absorb only a small proportion of a population, burst into such a flame throughout the country
that it affected in one way or another practically every
person in the community? How did the illegal practice gain its wide public support, in spite of the fact
that the dangerous smuggling gangs became a menace
to life and limb and committed atrocities beyond anything ever attempted by their predecessors, the owlers?
For a hundred and fifty years the English smuggler
was both a blessing and a curse to his country, securing
a strangle hold on the land from which it could not
shake itself. What was the cause of smuggling in this
grotesquely exaggerated form?

The original spark, of course, was the same as that
which had created the owlers—oppressive legislation—
but whereas the owlers only benefited one section of
the community in addition to themselves, the later
smugglers benefited practically every class. In that
fact lay their basic strength.

The smugglers had a splendid platform for appear-
ing as public benefactors. Money was needed for war
—itself far less popular than smuggling—and taxes on
commodities necessary for life and for the enjoyment
of life showered from the government as bitter manna
from heaven. It was no longer a question of hardship
on people who sheared sheep; it was a question of
hardship on everybody. The taxes hit England bang
in the stomach.

The housewife who had been taught to regard the
owlers as quite naughty people—very interesting to
talk about, and very entertaining to read about, but
very, very wrong—suddenly discovered that smugglers
could keep down her rising housekeeping bills and
preserve the good temper of her husband. The husband's good temper was also preserved by the thought,
as he took his nightcap, that thanks to the wicked
smugglers his bibulous instincts were not ruining him
—financially, anyway. The judge who punished the
smuggler when caught thanked him silently while
stirring his teacup. The M. P. who made laws to
frustrate him helped him (and himself) by smoking
contraband tobacco. The parson who preached against
him brought in the peace-proffered tub with the morning milk.

Even the riding officers, the revenue-cutter men, the soldiers, and the coast guards, when smuggling forced these latter into being, all received benefits directly or indirectly from the folk they were out to catch. No wonder a situation arose beyond the power, and often the will, of the authorities to check.

Spirits, wine, tea, tobacco, lace, silk, scent—to give the complete list of articles taxed to satisfy the voracious appetite of the war-machine would be tedious and numbing. The war-machine's appetite is never satisfied. Its mouth is wide open for gold as well as men.

The condition that was ultimately reached is most graphically and entertainingly described in the words of Sydney Smith, who issued a remarkable warning based on experience to the United States, when that country was on the verge of spending big sums to increase her navy.

We can inform Jonathan, he wrote, what are the inevitable consequences of being too fond of glory. Taxes upon every article which enters into the mouth, or covers the back, or is placed under the foot; taxes upon everything which it is pleasant to see, hear, feel, smell or taste; taxes upon warmth, light, and locomotion; taxes on everything on earth, and the waters under the earth; on everything that comes from abroad, or is grown at home; taxes on raw material, taxes on every fresh value that is added to it by the industry of man; taxes on the sauce which pampers man's appetite and the drug that restores him to health; on the ermine which decorates the judge and the rope which hangs the criminal; on the poor man's salt and the rich man's spice; on the brass nails of the coffin and the ribands of the bride; at bed or board, couchant or levant, we must pay.

Even that did not end the impassioned flow of an agonized taxpayer! Sidney Smith went on, developing his warning to its final swan song:

The schoolboy whips his taxed top; the beardless youth manages his taxed horse with a taxed bridle on a taxed road; and the dying Englishman, pouring his medicine, which has paid seven per cent, into a spoon that has paid fifteen per cent, flings himself back upon his chintz bed which has paid twenty-two per cent, makes his will on an eight-pound stamp, and expires in the arms of an apothecary who has paid a license of a hundred pounds for the privilege of putting him to death. His whole property is then immediately taxed from two to ten per cent. Besides the probate, large fees are demanded for burying him in the chancel; his virtues are handed down to posterity on taxed marble; and he is then gathered to his fathers—to be taxed no more.

The one happy conclusion we may draw from Sidney Smith's depressing list is that, no matter how much an Englishman is taxed, he does not lose his sense of humor. But his smile does not dispel his suffering, and the taxpayer suffered very considerably during the great smuggling era that arose to ease him.

The smugglers estimated, and facts proved the estimate to be approximately correct, that if they landed and disposed of one cargo out of three they cleared a profit. This reckoning included the loss of such boats as were seized and subjected to the penalty of being sawed into three parts, for since the builders were alive to the risks their boats would run, they built them as economically as was consistent with efficiency. Frequently the period between the sighting and the capture of a smuggling boat—if indeed the capture were effected at all—was sufficient to allow the smugglers time to save the cargo by one or other of their ingenious methods. A favorite device was to "sink" a cargo and to regain it later—though not too much later, unless necessity forced delaying the operation, since if certain liquors soaked in brine for many hours they gained, and richly deserved, the title of "stinkibus." The title conveys their condition when recovered. But when a valuable cargo was preserved by "sinking" and regained in good condition, the loss of the boat that brought it was often a matter of comparative unimportance.

Often, but not always. Some of the smuggling vessels were worth considerable, and by their speed and seaworthiness, as well as by their traditions, earned famous names for themselves. To mention the *Two Brothers*, for instance, or the *Daniel and William*, with its two complete sets of different-colored sails to cheat identification, or the *Sarah Jacobe*, as changeable as a woman because it could transform its appearance at will into that of a cutter, sloop, dandy or trawler, was to plant in the eyes of the smuggler a light of pride as great as any felt by the modern Briton in the *Queen Mary*.

Smugglers were quite as clever in the art of boat-building as they were in the art of handling the boats they built, and many local fleets stood high in their peculiar distinction. If you wanted the best boat for a spot of smuggling you would not go to the Clyde. You would go to Looe, Mevagissey, Cawsand or Polperro.

Of course the boat-builders and the boat-users merely formed a portion, if the most skillful portion, of the whole smuggling organization. In a complete run, from the foreign port where the contraband was bought cheaply to the spot in Great Britain where it was sold not quite so cheaply, but sufficiently cheaply to find an eager market, the majority of workers were the land-smugglers, or porters or tub-carriers, as they were alternatively called. These formed for the most part the short-time, unskilled helpers, whose duty it was to convey the contraband from the coast and to cheat the vigilance of the excisemen on land, as the boatmen had cheated the revenue cutters on sea. It was largely because the freighters, or principals, had such a big and willing army of unskilled labor to draw upon that their industry thrived.

Where did the unskilled labor come from? This in itself is a point of considerable interest.

The country at this time was particularly full of dissatisfied or unhappy people. Taxes were not the only oppressions that exerted an unsettling influence. Wars and revolutions were filling minds with fears and uneasiness, and both the power and the virtue of authority were being discredited. Lawlessness spread because those responsible for the law seemed unable to control it or point to its good works, and in this atmosphere people with the weakest principles were easily swayed.

Unemployment was rife. There was no dole in those days. If you hadn't a job, the Army or the Navy might gather you into its net, for while taxes swallowed money, the press gangs swallowed people without any. The human derelicts went through a thin time.

But smuggling offered, to the majority of them, a new trade. Not the furtive trade of lonely criminality, but the organized trade of a vast community of criminals, anomalously backed by half the country it was fleecing. A trade to which you could be apprenticed. Occupation, pay, organization, social intercourse, power—these things were offered to the derelicts by the smuggling fraternity, with plenty of adventure and free liquor and 'baccy! All you had to do was to close your eyes to that vague ideal of Right—if your eyes had ever been opened—to be on a certain spot when summoned, to march, hit, and carry, and to obey simple orders.

"And don't forget, my lad," winked the smuggler's recruiting officer, "'tis good work to fight against bad laws, and who likes taxes?"

And so the derelicts and down-and-outs, the deserters and convicts, the well-to-do who had fallen on evil times, the youngest sons of youngest sons, and the flotsam and jetsam of a sorely confused age became porters and tub-carriers, escaping from the press gangs

under the smugglers' protective wing. And all had
their chance of rising in their new and "honorable"
profession.

There was irony as well as ambiguity in their title
of free traders, since when Free Trade came along it
dimmed their glory. They preferred the title of "fair
traders," and were generally under the impression that
they deserved it. Thickest at first in Kent and Sussex,
owing to the proximity of these counties to the Continent, the contrabandists quickly spread round the
coast in both directions, till the geographical definition
of Britain could aptly have been changed to "an island
surrounded by smugglers."

They had centers inland, however, as well as on
the coast, and some of the worst elements formed
themselves into notorious groups. The smuggling
gangs, of which the Hawkhurst Gang was probably
the most famous—or infamous—provide some of the
most thrilling, and also most terrible, pages in smuggling history.

One reason why the British government took so
many generations to organize successfully against
smuggling was the service performed by the contraband merchants to a vast section of the community,
but another reason was its absorption in other matters
equally grave. The wars that had indirectly given the
smugglers their excuse and their opportunity prevented
the government from developing its defense against
its internal foes, and not until the Battle of Waterloo
was it free to turn its full attention from the greater
evil to the lesser. Even then about half a century was

needed before it could claim to have "made a job of it."

Meanwhile, of course, it received plenty of well-meant advice from amateur politicians. Human nature was much the same then as it is today. One of the brightest proposals was advanced by an earnest individual who urged a tax of from five to twenty shillings on all tea-drinking families. Even if this fresh burden had been added to the tea-drinker, it is difficult to see how it could have put the tea-smuggler out of business. It would merely have made the government more unpopular than it already was!

So the proposal was ignored, with many another, and smuggling went merrily on.

From a correspondent's letter in the *Gentleman's Magazine*, September 3, 1735:

"In several parts of Kent the farmers are obliged to raise wages, and are yet distressed for want of hands to get in their harvest, which is attributed to the great numbers who employ themselves in smuggling along the coast."

(One ultimate result of this situation was a shortage of bread. The royal family cut out pastry, and the Archbishop of Canterbury begged all good Christians to do likewise.)

Smuggling Gangs

F
O R the greater portion of the eighteenth century, smuggling gangs terrorized the English countryside.

It was obvious that this should be so. The law was grasping but impotent, and to provide the criminal with temptation, without at the same time providing sufficient policemen to catch him, is just asking for trouble. Finding their strength, the smugglers increased it. Individuals banded together, elected for their leaders the cleverest, the most daring, and the least scrupulous, and established local "armies" against which the authorities, as a rule, were powerless.

These gangs, as they expanded, did not confine themselves entirely to the business of smuggling, although trading in contraband was, of course, the primary cause of their being. But a great contraband war was on, a war that was most rampant in the south of England but that extended northward far into Scotland, and in order to win their countless victories the smugglers had to plot, plan, spy, fight and terrorize. They were particularly successful at the latter.

The dragoons and excisemen, pitifully few in number—as a rule the smugglers outnumbered them by ten to one—had to be watched and their habits and movements secretly studied. Information regarding contraband and impending "runs" had to be gained and spread in the necessary quarters. Informers, those hated outcasts, had to be marked and dealt with. Fresh recruits had to be secured. And, incidentally, as the smuggling prospered, other crimes were added to the list, though these were usually accomplished by the more degraded individuals and gangs. In spite of the terror they spread, and often delighted in spreading, it must be remembered that the average smuggler clung to his queer ethics and insisted that he was right in what he did.

You might have to bind and gag an exciseman—certainly. You might have to knock him out—certainly. You might have to kill him. Without any doubt whatever, you might have to kill or torture an informer, blast his miserable bones! But that was war, wasn't it? And people were killing each other at sea and on the Continent, weren't they? Why, that was at the bottom of the whole trouble. And, the smugglers concluded their argument, if the press gang got

them, or if they were caught and punished with five
years' service on a warship, they'd have to kill, anyway
—so what was the difference?

Even more than good laws, humble folk need good
examples. Lacking both, the smuggling gangs went
on their way.

Gray's men—Morten's men—the Hawkhurst Gang
—the Ruxley Gang—these were among the many
household words that merely had to be mentioned to
send timid people at dusk hurrying indoors, pulling
curtains across their small diamond-paned windows, or
extinguishing their lamps or candles.

Something was afoot! They might eventually
profit by it, but they did not want to get mixed up in
it. Wasn't this the night named in the anonymous
letter opened not long since by the farmer up the lane?
The message had demanded that all the farmer's
horses should be ready and waiting, unattended, for
the smugglers, and it was as certain that the farmer
was obeying his bashful correspondent as it was that
the horses would in due course be returned to him with
a couple of untapped casks. The smugglers paid their
way—or burned the house of the farmer who refused
to do business with them.

Behind the drawn curtain, in the dimness of their
little parlor, the timid people wait. Their ears are
strained for sounds upon the road. It will be a tramp-
tramp-tramp. The tramp of perhaps a hundred burly,
hard-muscled men. Some of the men will be the
porters, each with two four-gallon casks, one slung in
front and one behind. The porter who trips will roll.

If the lugger that brought over the brandy had a full cargo, and the whole cargo was successfully landed, the number of porters will be forty. The others with them will be the leaders and the batmen—the armed guard. The batmen will not be carrying casks but cudgels, iron implements, rakes, knives, perhaps even firearms. A pity they've started using those things. . . .

As the timid people listen, one of them continually misses his swallow, then bites the inside of his lip till it bleeds. The others do not look at him. They dare not, for they suspect the reason of his particular paleness. They saw him, only that morning, talking to an exciseman.

"Here they come!"

"Sh!"

"Lord above!"

Now the tramp is faintly heard upon the road. First, like a distant whisper of approaching feet. Then a steady, regular augmenting noise. Tramp-tramp, tramp-tramp, tramp-tramp. The marchers do not sing "Yo, heave-ho, and a bottle of rum!" The journey of French brandy is a silent one, save for the sound of those heavy, funereal feet. Four-gallon casks, after a mile or two, get heavy.

But the tramp will change to a clatter when the procession reaches the horses waiting, unattended, in the farmyard at the end of the lane. That is, unless . . . The timid listener with the palest face suddenly finds that his knees have given way beneath him, and that he is sitting on the floor.

Others in the village also hear the smugglers tramp by. A saucy girl grows bold, pulls her curtain aside, and winks at one of the porters. He catches sight of her and winks back. She will get her share.

A batman pauses and turns his head to get a glimpse of the village Venus. The man behind blunders into him with a pitchfork. An angry oath breaks the silence of the night.

Then the tramping passes its crescendo, diminishes, becomes a whisper again, fades out. Nothing stirs. There is perfect stillness. The listeners wait for the next sound. The clatter of horses' hooves.

But the silence is not broken by horses' hooves. It is broken by sudden shouts and cries, and a loud report.

Two days later, the farm is in flames, and the man whose knees gave way is missing.

The smugglers never lost an opportunity to repay what they regarded as treachery. Whether they won or were beaten in a surprise encounter with the exciseman—and they generally won—they sought the cause of the leakage and meted out their particular form of punishment. If the farmer or any other person was suspected of having reported the demand for the horses, no mercy was shown to either.

In 1746 the distracted authorities themselves instituted a unique form of punishment. They punished counties. For the seizure of contraband minus the smugglers, the "offending" county was fined two hundred pounds. The fine was remitted, however, if the smugglers were captured during the succeeding six months. Thus smuggler-hunting became a sort of game in which you played for your county, though the danger of the game rather reduced the team spirit.

For a revenue officer who was killed, the fine paid by
the county in which he died was one hundred pounds.
There was no remission of that, since the dead officer
could not be brought to life again. The figure was
hardly flattering to the revenue officer, whose death
was financially assessed as representing half the damage of that caused by running goods. For a few
bruises only, the fine was forty pounds.

These fines formed the negative side of England's
attempt to urge law-abiding folk to become smuggler-
chasers. The positive side was a standing reward of
five hundred pounds for a smuggler's capture.

That the hard-working excisemen needed more assistance than they were getting was very obvious. At
this period there were only a few hundred customs
officers, with about the same number of dragoons—
most of them unwilling—to lend them a hand. There
was a disgraceful lack of co-operation between the excisemen and the soldiers, and permission to make use
of the latter was often the subject of protracted cor-
respondence which was certainly not the excisemen's
fault. The Army, thinking a lot of itself in spite of
the fact that the dragoons were more easily bribed
than the excisemen, would not unbend until quite
satisfied that the need existed; and, as likely as not, by
the time they discovered that the need had existed, it
existed no longer.

Even when trouble still remained to be dealt with,
the methods employed were sometimes suspiciously
unsuccessful. The dragoons let many a smuggler slip
through their fingers, and strong excisemen were too
frequently found bound and gagged. Unready to die

or even to suffer for their job, some of them yielded to fear or temptation, and allowed themselves to be bound and gagged without any protest. It is recorded on the yellowest pages of history that a few actually asked for the indignity, receiving a subsequent gift for having advanced the convenient request. The honest exciseman, therefore, who was discovered helpless, always had difficulty in proving that he had done his best but that the best had not been good enough. As a rule he was dismissed either for inefficiency or for cheating. It was thankless work.

The greatest scourge of the times was the notorious Hawkhurst Gang, which, under Arthur Gray, was terrorizing the country east of Tunbridge Wells. On a bleak December day in 1744, the gang suddenly attacked a very small band of customs men, severely wounded the commander, and took their prisoners to Hawkhurst. Two of the prisoners were ex-smugglers who had "turned honest"—perhaps! They were roped to trees and mercilessly beaten. Then their almost dead bodies were carted to the coast, and a smuggler's boat conveyed them to France, to continue there what life still existed. A special reward of fifty pounds offered for "bringing the persons concerned to justice" was never, apparently, claimed.

Three months later the Hawkhurst Gang swarmed into a public house at Grimstead Green, wounded and flogged three officers who were drinking there, and left them *sans* timepieces—and gold pieces. From this it will be seen that the gangs were extending the scope of their activities.

It is with relief that we turn to the epic of Goud-

IN THE HANDS OF THE HAWKHURST GANG

hurst. Grim though it is, a refreshing atmosphere of real heroism runs through it to revive our tottering faith in humanity.

Goudhurst is about four miles north of Hawkhurst, and its inhabitants had suffered severely under this reign of terror. If the government could do nothing, Goudhurst itself would have a shot at it, taking defense in its own hands as the smuggling gangs were taking the law. The name of the hero of this episode is variously given as Stuart and Sturt. Stout would better describe him, the reference being to his heart, not his figure. His figure must have been normal, since he was a young man of vigorous activity.

When Goudhurst had had about as much as it could stand, Stuart called a meeting of the honest men round him, and together they drew up a document in which they expressed their horror and indignation at the smugglers' atrocities, and their firm intention of ending them. It was a bold gesture, backed by a bold signature. The document was signed, "The Goudhurst Militia."

Stuart, born in Goudhurst, had served in a foot regiment, so he was qualified by both birth and experience to be their leader.

The Hawkhurst Gang heard of the document and laughed. An upstart called Stuart, with a handful of timid, inexperienced villagers, was going to set himself up against such names as Arthur Gray and Thomas Kingsmill and the greatest gang in the kingdom. By all the terrible things by which the Hawkhurst Gang swore, this was funny!

The first point was scored by the Hawkhurst men.

They captured a member of the newly formed Militia, tortured him—they were experts in despicable methods of applying pressure—and obtained such information as he could supply. The information did not worry them in the least. They sent the unfortunate victim back to Goudhurst with an impudent message to deliver. On such and such a day, Goudhurst was to prepare for its doom. It would be attacked, burned to the ground, and every inhabitant murdered.

Hawkhurst did not know the metal Goudhurst was made of. When the message from the enemy was duly delivered, Stuart called another meeting, not of protest this time, but of preparation. The threat might be an empty threat, but smugglers generally meant what they said, and the Goudhurst Militia did not intend to be caught napping.

In the regular army Stuart had been last in Rome. Now he was first in a village, and he gave the village all his army knowledge. The Goudhurst Militia had very little equipment, but they spent the interim in adding to it, combing the neighborhood for firearms or any other kind of weapon they could find. Such

lead as they could gather was made into balls for the muskets. Defenses were erected, and behind these the Militia waited.

In due course the Hawkhurst Gang turned up in strong force. They meant business, and had as their leader Thomas Kingsmill, already a name to shrink from, and destined, in another affair, to become even more terrifying. The attackers began by demanding unconditional surrender. The Militia refused the suggestion. Then the smugglers opened fire, and were astounded to find the fire returned. One of their men fell dead.

Amazed and cursing, the Hawkhurst Gang fired again, but the homemade bullets of the homemade army proved better and more accurate than the smugglers'. More attackers fell, two not to rise again, and as the Goudhurst Militia saw the confusion they had sown they left their defenses and became themselves attackers.

The smugglers fled. They left behind them several wounded and three dead. One of the dead was George Kingsmill, the leader's brother. It was a pity for the future that George, and not Thomas, was chosen to stop a bullet. Thomas fled with the rest, and presumably among the fastest; for many captures were made, but Thomas Kingsmill was not among the prisoners.

By all the justice of poetry, that should have been the end of the Hawkhurst Gang. Unfortunately it was not. They lived to play a part in the famous attack on the customhouse at Poole, and in the dastardly episodes that followed it.

A SMUGGLER'S EPITAPH
(In the churchyard of Kinson, Dorset)

To the memory of Robert Trotman, late of Rowd, in the county of Wilts, who was barbarously murdered on the shore near Poole, the 24th March, 1765.

A little tea, one leaf I did not steal,
For guiltless bloodshed I to God appeal;
Put tea in one scale, human blood in t'other,
And think what 'tis to slay a harmless brother.

Galley and Chater

T H I S is a terrible tale. It is probably the cruelest to be found in the smugglers' bag, and it is not recommended to those who avoid "thrill" stories for the sake of their health. But no history of smuggling would be complete without this grim epic which began in Guernsey in September, 1747, and ended with seven death-sentences at Chichester in January, 1749, and it will not be told here in the language of the "Gentleman of Chichester" who, in 1752, published a best-seller under the hardly snappy title of *A Full and Genuine History of the Inhuman and Unparalleled Murders of Mr. William Galley and Mr. Daniel Chater by Fourteen Notorious Smugglers.*

There is an insistent unction in the title—one can

almost visualize the Gentleman of Chichester rolling
it out!—that is reflected in the painfully elaborate details of the story itself. As many of these details as
possible will be omitted from the present version.

The tale begins as hundreds of other smuggling
tales have begun—with the purchase of tea in Guernsey. It was a large purchase, and the boat that left
Guernsey had a cargo of thirty-seven hundredweight,
representing a value of five hundred pounds. Far too
good a cargo to lose. But, unfortunately for more
persons than the smugglers themselves, they did lose
it. A revenue cutter spotted the smuggling craft in
the Channel, chased it, and caught it. The credit for
this unusual success went to Captain Johnson, who
proudly conveyed the tea to Poole and had it locked
up in the customhouse there.

A public sale should have been the end of it. Unfortunately, however, the smugglers could not bear the
idea of losing five hundred pounds, and they decided
to smash the customhouse open before the sale took
place.

They laid their plans with military precision, met
on the night of October 6 in Charlton Forest, and divided into two armies. One army marched to the
harbor to do the work, while the other army spread
itself out to make sure that the work was not interrupted.

If any riding officers had been abroad that night,
some of them would not have seen another sunrise,
for the smugglers were fully armed, and were in a
mood to use their weapons. But no officers appeared.
Either they considered the tea safe, or decided to keep

themselves so. While thirty men watched, thirty more battered, and soon after midnight they had smashed the door down and were bringing thirty-seven hundredweight of tea onto the quay.

The return journey, begun in the cold gray hours, was concluded in broad daylight, and as the horsemen processioned through Fordingbridge the villagers turned out to admire them. One of the villagers was a shoemaker who would have done better to stick to his last. His name was Daniel Chater.

Chater had been a farm-laborer before he took to the shoe business, and he suddenly recognized an old friend among the smugglers. John Diamond had also been a farm-laborer, and had changed *his* job less reputably. The two friends smiled at each other and shook hands; and before he passed on, Diamond tossed Chater a bag of tea.

It was amazing that the smugglers could indulge in such publicity and get away with it. When in due course the raid was discovered and rewards were offered for identifying the miscreants, not one among those who had seen them came forward. Those who did not love the smugglers feared them.

But one smuggler was arrested on suspicion. This was Diamond, who had tossed Chater the tea. Chater, unable to curb his tongue, may have talked too much before his old friend's arrest; he certainly talked too much after. In order that he should talk more, the collector of customs at Southampton interviewed him, and he agreed to go and see a Major Battin, who was a justice of peace and commissioner of customs at Chichester.

Whatever we may think of smugglers, and our opinion will not improve as this story proceeds, we may also think that Chater was asking for trouble in offering to identify the man who had presented him with a packet of tea. For that was the main object of the projected visit to Chichester, and the identification would mean the donor's death. Incidentally, in addition to having received tea from the smuggler, Chater would receive another award for having helped to give the smuggler to the gallows.

Still, we need not disarm our sympathy for Chater as we watch him mount his horse for Chichester. He was probably just a poor fool, demoralized like countless others by the times. There will certainly be no lack of sympathy for his companion on this ride. William Galley, an excise officer, was deputed to accompany him, and Galley's sheet was completely clean.

The day on which they took the fatal ride was Valentine's Day, 1748, five months after the attack on the Poole customhouse. Events had moved slowly since then, but now they moved faster. At Havant an acquaintance of Chater's sealed his doom by advising the riders to continue through Stanstead, near Rowland's Castle. They lost their road, but were put on it again when they inquired at the New Inn, Leigh. Three men from the inn then accompanied them. They no longer journeyed alone.

Tea was the start of the trouble. Rum led to the end of it. If the riders had not felt thirsty when at last they reached Rowland's Castle, they would not have stopped at the White Hart for a drink. Unfortunately for two of them, the White Hart was owned by a Mrs. Payne, whose two sons were blacksmiths on top and smugglers at bottom.

Mrs. Payne always suspected strangers, and while Chater and Galley were drinking she drew one of their companions aside and asked whether they were all right. Meaning, of course, all wrong. The man assured her they were harmless. They were merely taking a letter to Major Battin, he said, and there was nothing to worry about.

It is difficult at this distance of time to understand how much simplicity existed in the midst of subtlety. Why did Chater mention to strangers that he was carrying a letter to a commissioner of customs at Chichester? He knew its contents, and he was in smuggling territory. Throughout this sorry business Chater appears to have shown a most stupid lack of suspicion, and to have infected his traveling companion with his own germ of folly. And why did Mrs. Payne's informant assume that the letter had no connection with smuggling?

Up to this point, Mrs. Payne herself was the only member who acted with intelligence, however crooked that intelligence was. The mere mention of Major Battin caused her suspicious eyes to sharpen, and she sent one of her sons to bring along two smugglers who were in the neighborhood, and who were wanted considerably more urgently than was John Diamond. "If there's any trouble brewing," ran her thought, "Jackson and Carter will know how to handle it!"

Jackson and Carter had both been in the Poole affair, and they were blackguards with very definite ideas of how to handle trouble.

While her son was away, the two unsuspecting guests laid down their empty glasses and asked for their horses. It really was most unfortunate, Mrs. Payne told them, but the horses were locked in the stable, and the man with the key was out. But he would be back before long, if the gentlemen would not mind waiting.

Whether they minded or not, they had to wait. They filled in the time pleasantly enough. It is always agreeable to drink and chat.

Then Mrs. Payne's son returned with Jackson and Carter, and shortly afterward her second son brought four more smugglers along. This made the odds eight men to two against Galley and Chater. The three men from Leigh are not included, for one of them left the inn hurriedly when he was warned that clouds were gathering, while the other two drowned whatever apprehensions they may have had in drink. None of these had any hand in what followed.

Acting in a friendly way, Jackson asked Chater for a few words in private and took him into the yard. Chater, ever a simpleton, fell into the simplest of traps. Once more he could not keep his tongue quiet, and by now liquor was helping it to wag. Yes, he was going to Chichester. Yes, to see Major Battin. Certainly, about John Diamond. Well, naturally he had a letter. Where? In his pocket, of course . . .

Meanwhile Galley noted the absence of his companion, and went into the yard rather anxiously to see what was happening. Jackson promptly bashed him in the face and knocked him down.

"I am a King's officer, and cannot put up with such

treatment!" cried Galley; and behaving very unlike a King's officer, he picked himself up, and fled back to the inn.

Jackson followed him, obviously intending to continue the treatment, but one of Mrs. Payne's sons told him not to be a fool. Jackson suddenly altered his tactics and apologized.

The unexpected apology was accepted. Joined by the trembling Chater, Galley said once more that they must go. And now they committed their final act of folly. Probably they would not have been allowed to go in any case, but instead of using their wits or making a fight of it, the two men yielded to apparently friendly protests and sat down to final health-drinking. The healths proved the last Galley and Chater ever drank.

In a few minutes they were helpless with liquor. They staggered into an adjoining room to sleep it off. When they were dead to the world, the smugglers relieved them of their damning letters and went into conference.

They were joined at the conference by two more smugglers, John Race and Richard Kelly, and also by the wives of Jackson and Carter. Such men found wives somehow, and the wives often became as bad as the men. The two women plumped promptly for hanging.

Of three other suggestions, two were more gentle. The first was to transport Galley and Chater to France. That idea was knocked on the head by the thought that they would probably find their way back again. The second was to keep them in some secret place till the fate of Diamond became known, the smugglers meanwhile each paying threepence per week for the prisoners' upkeep. That idea was knocked on the head because no one, apart from the proposer, was ready to pay threepence a week to keep such scum alive. The third suggestion had no gentleness in it, and was therefore more popular—to kill them and drop them down a well. One was handy.

Before a decision was reached, Jackson's brutality got the better of him. He dashed into the next room to begin the torture, kicking the drunken victims into painful consciousness and digging the spur of his riding boot into their faces. When they had managed to stagger to their feet, they were whipped out of the room back into the kitchen.

The smugglers had tasted blood, and reverted to the law of the jungle. They sank lower than the jungle, for wild beasts lack the advantage of a human mind to check their savagery. The terrified men were carried out and bound together on a horse, and while the horse bore them through the dark lanes—for night had set in—they were whipped and lashed continuously.

One of the smugglers brandished a cocked pistol to frighten any wayfarers away.

The brutal journey continued till 2 A.M., when the party reached the Red Lion Inn at Rake, on the Portsmouth Road. (Gentled into a cottage, the Red Lion stands today.) The innkeeper's name was Scardefield, and when he descended in response to the smugglers' knocking, he discovered that he had reversed the usual process and awakened into a night-

mare. Jackson explained the nightmare by saying that
they had fallen in with a band of King's officers, and
that they had brought in a couple of casualties.

The innkeeper served the required refreshment and
asked no questions.

The victims, unfortunately for them, were not quite
dead, but Galley was finished off that night. He was
buried in Harting Combe, in circumstances which
shall not be described. Those who want the description—it is not recommended—will find it in the account written by the "Gentleman of Chichester."

With even more cruelty, poor Chater was allowed
to live on for a while, and was temporarily confined
in a turf-shed of one Richard Mills. Then the murderous gang returned home, getting back before sunrise, and arranging to foregather again at the Red
Lion in a couple of days.

Richard Mills and his son went through an anxious

period meanwhile. The only sympathy they felt was for themselves. They did not want Chater's body found on their premises.

There were fourteen men at the next conference at the Red Lion. One by one, when the normal business of the day was over, they slipped casually into the kitchen. Mills was, of course, among them, for he now had an anxious interest in the matter, and he made a suggestion which was worthy of a modern mystery writer. The words quoted are declared by the "Gentleman of Chichester" to have been spoken by Mills, but probably that uneducated individual used a simpler phraseology. The language smacks rather too much of the accomplished master-mind:

"Let us load a gun with two or three bullets," ran the alleged speech, "lay it upon a stand with the muzzle of the piece levelled at his head, and, after having tied a long strong to the trigger we will all go off to the butt-end, and, each of us taking hold of the string, pull it all together; thus we shall be all equally guilty of his death, and it will be impossible for any one of us to charge the rest with his murder, without accusing himself of the same crime; and none can pretend to lessen or to mitigate his guilt by saying he was only an accessory, since all will be principals."

Such was the gist, in any case, of Mills's oration.

His one thought was to safeguard his own skin by attaching it, in terms of guilt, to the skins of the rest, and he deserves high marks for ingenuity, if for nothing else. But the meeting decided that shooting would be too merciful. For the final verdict, and the manner in which the verdict was carried out, the patient reader is again referred, with a warning, to the "Gentleman of Chichester." The warning may gain color when it is added that this pamphlet was written in the days when people flocked to public hangings for the pleasure of them, and feasted their shuddering eyes on pirates and smugglers hanging in chains.

After almost incredible tortures, endured at the turf-shed and at Lady Holt Park some five miles distant, Chater ended what remained of his life down a well.

Having now got rid of the two men, the blackguards thought, rather late, of their victims' horses, which had been locked up at the White Hart Inn. Returning there, they brought the horses out, killed one and cut it up, and then turned round to find the other missing. That is one of the few bright spots in this gruesome tale!

If the tale were fiction and not fact, the horse would obviously have galloped riderless into Chichester, stopped outside Major Battin's door, and mutely told its story. There would have been blood on the saddle, with a clue to those who had shed it. But as the horse vanished from the White Hart Inn, so it vanished from history, and the first clue to the tragedy was the finding of Galley's bloodstained greatcoat near Rowland's Castle. This, coupled with the absence of the wearer and of Chater, confirmed dawning suspicions of foul play, and the government offered a free pardon to anyone who would confess and bring the ringleaders to justice.

It was about seven months, however, before an anonymous letter was received, naming a certain per-

son and mentioning where he could be called on.
The reason for the long delay was not that people
lacked information, but that they were unwilling or
afraid to give it. We may quote a passage from the
Chichester Gentleman's account to indicate the dark
spell which the smugglers had cast over the land:

The terrible executions committed by the
smugglers on these poor men, and the dreadful
menaces which they uttered against any person
that should presume to interrupt them, so terrified the people everywhere, that scarce anybody
durst look at them as they passed in large bodies
in open daylight. And the customs officers were
so intimidated that hardly any of them had courage enough to go on their duty. Some of them
they knew they had already sent to France, others
had been killed or wounded in opposing them,
and Galley, in particular, had been inhumanly
murdered by them.

The smugglers had reigned a long time un-
controlled; they rode in troops to fetch their
goods, and carried them off in triumph by daylight; nay, so audacious were they grown, that
they were not afraid of regular troops that were
sent into the country to keep them in awe, of
which we have had several instances. If any one
of them happened to be taken, and the proof ever
so clear against him, no magistrate in the county
durst commit him to gaol; if he did, he was sure
to have his house or his barns set on fire, or some
other mischief done him if he was so happy to
escape with his life.

This contemporary commentator did not under-
paint his picture. We may hope that, in certain details, he overpainted it. In any case, after seven months

of hesitation, somebody started the ball of justice rolling, and it continued to roll until it had rolled out seven ruffians, including Jackson and Carter. The individual named in the anonymous letter was arrested and turned King's evidence. The arrests of the worst of the culprits followed, and on January 16, 1749, they were tried and found guilty.

A few days later, views near Rake, on the Portsmouth Road, Rook's Hill, Chichester, and the seacoast by Selsea Bill were marred by figures hanging in chains.

Jackson's was not among them. The cruelest of the lot, he proved the greatest coward when it came to his own skin. In a book no less gloomy than the Gentleman of Chichester's, and frankly entitled *Hanging in Chains*, the author, Mr. Harkhorne, says of William Jackson:

> He, also, was condemned to be hung, and gibbeted in chains; but the poor wretch was so ill, and horror-struck when they measured him for his irons, that he died of fright.

His worthless body was tossed into a hole. The worms must have shuddered.

Printed paper, supposed to be a "Popish relique," found sewn in a purse in Jackson's waistcoat pocket after he was captured:

Ye three Holy Kings,
Gaspar, Melchior, Balthasar,
Pray for us now, and in the hour of death.

The papers have touched the three heads of the Holy Kings at Cologne. They are to preserve travelers from accidents on the roads, headaches, falling sickness, fever, witchcraft, all kinds of mischief and sudden death.

Carter, Carter, Carter & Carter

SOMETIMES fame comes to the individual, sometimes to the family. The Carters, of Prussia Cove, Cornwall, probably deserve to be ranked as Smuggling Family No. One.

There were a dozen of them—father, mother, eight sons, and two daughters. Carter Senior came from Shropshire, but he settled in Cornwall in the middle of the eighteenth century, and his children were born with the tang of the sea and the smell of the rocky, seaweedy coast in their nostrils. As they grew up they played "King of the Castle" on the beach, and John, the eldest, was always the king. The particular monarch he emulated was Frederick the Great, King of

Prussia, and this is how the cove in which they played obtained its ephemeral name. John being the King of Prussia, he had to christen the sandy region he ruled over appropriately.

Prussia Cove was an isolated little bay between Helston and Marazion, but it was not in sight of either, or of the highroad that ran between the two towns. It was practically inaccessible from the road saving to those who—like the Carters themselves—knew the tortuous cliff-tracks, while rocks and overhanging cliffs camouflaged its existence from the sea. No spot more snug could have been chosen for secret enterprises.

The Carter children did not choose it; they grew up in it; and they grew up as well to the idea of smuggling, which was as natural to them as football or cricket is to the schoolboy of today. These were the days when even country parsons closed their eyes to "these dreadful goings on," and received embarrassing gifts for doing so. They were also the days of the Cornish wreckers, who lured ships onto the treacherous rocks for the plunder they derived from the wreckages. Born and bred in the thick of all this, the Carter children followed the practices of their neighborhod and times, but they seem to have kept out of the worst offenses. They were not wreckers. While all profited by smuggling, and probably all indulged in it, it was only the four eldest boys—John, Francis Junior, Henry and Charles—who became real experts, and although everybody knew that the Carters did not make their money in farming and fishing, or in running the stone house they built on a shelf overlooking the cove as an inn, they were respected even by the excise officers themselves. They were, according to their lights, honest smugglers, and they were not cruel.

Here is one example of John's honesty. John remained "King of the Castle" after he grew up, and was the accepted leader of the family band. His movements therefore held a special interest for the excisemen, who learned one day that he was away from home, and paid a special visit to see what they could find in his absence. They found much good liquor. It had recently been landed, and no duty had been paid on it. When John returned, he found that every keg had been taken away to the customhouse at Penzance.

John did not blame the excisemen. They had to do their duty if he would not pay his. But he had to get those kegs back, in order to keep faith with his customers. They were not his personal property. The Carters financed some of their enterprises, but they had "sleeping partners" farther inland who supplied a good part of the funds of their trade.

He went to Penzance that night. He broke into the customhouse. He found his kegs, and he brought them all back to his cove—in order that he might keep faith with his clients. (To keep faith with a government three hundred miles away was a shadowy matter.) But—and this was the point that impressed the local authorities—he also kept faith with the excisemen. He could have brought away countless other kegs that lay temptingly in the customhouse. He only brought away his own. For this surprising restraint in an age of dishonesty, he was named "Honest John Carter."

Another incident, of a more startling nature, reflected official tolerance at its conclusion.

With more audacity than was probably wise, John introduced some small cannon into his front garden. His less daring brothers may have regarded these new acquisitions as intriguing toys, but one day John used the toys, and opened fire upon a revenue sloop, the *Fairy*. His excuse was that the sloop was chasing a smugglers' boat, and was sending a party to land in the cove. The astonished landing party turned round and went back to the sloop, which departed as fast as possible, so that it could live to fight another day.

John's surprising behavior was duly reported, and the next morning a small army of mounted soldiers called to demand an explanation. John objected to the call, and when the soldiers opened fire, the family quickly retired to the only other building in the neighborhood—an inn in the next cove named, somewhat frivolously, the "Kidleywink." Possibly the good lady who owned this inn—Bessie Burrow—had a comic streak in her nature. But comic or not, she was a friend in need, and she allowed the Carters to use her house as a sanctuary, even though the soldiers, armed with muskets and now in possession of John's cannon, might come along and demolish it.

The soldiers did not come. The Carters waited for the army to arrive and complete its victory, but the army was disposed to let the battle remain a bloodless one—and turned round and went back to Penzance!

On the previous day, the Carters had made a revenue boat run away. Now the Carters themselves had been made to run away. Honor was satisfied. John was not even summoned for his original most improper behavior. As it was not repeated, perhaps the authorities understood their man.

Although John was the leader of the "four musketeers"—John, Francis, Henry and Charles—Henry was the most interesting character, and he left behind him a picturesque account of his life. His *Autobiography of a Cornish Smuggler*, written after he had given up smuggling for more saintly ways, is well worth reading. It does more than paint a picture of the times; it reveals the writer as a very unusual psychological study.

"Captain Harry," as he was called, had no idea that smuggling was wrong when he began it. He took to the practice as a duck takes to water. But John Wesley was becoming an influence in the neighborhood, and was changing Cornwall's moral outlook. Wesleyan Methodist meetinghouses were springing up everywhere, and in due course they worried Captain Harry. He wavered backward and forward, and then forward and backward, on a tide of circumstances too confusing for his simple mind. In the end he was "converted," but it was after much wavering and backsliding.

When he was seventeen, he informs us, he joined his brothers in fishing and smuggling. The fishing grew less, and the smuggling more, till at the age of twenty-five he was carrying on a regular smuggling trade in a ten-ton sloop. Being successful "rather beyond common," in his own terms, he gave up the ten-ton sloop for a twenty-ton sloop, which was specially built for him. Then followed a thirty-ton cutter, requiring a crew of ten. "I sailed in her one year," says his autobiography, "and I suppose made more safe voyages than have ever been made, since or before, with any single person."

Captain Harry should have been perfectly happy. He was only happy in part. He had that troublesome thing called a conscience, and though it must be admitted that he did not attend to it at this time, it paid him out for his neglect. Unlike the majority of smugglers, who believed that they were taking bad laws into their own hands and readjusting social injustices, Harry could not get it out of his head that he was doing wrong, and those Methodist meetinghouses were the devil of a nuisance! But if they disturbed his mind they did not disturb his business, for "in the course of these few years," he writes, "as we card a large trade with other vessels allso, we gained a large sum of money, and being a speculating family, was not satisfied with small things."

But then—in December, 1777—came catastrophe.

Dissatisfied with small things, and now regarding thirty tons as on the small side, the Carters acquired a cutter of twice that tonnage, and Captain Harry took

her with uneasy pride across the wide Channel. She was a boat to be proud of, for she had sixteen guns; but a bowsprit gave trouble, and she went into St. Malo for repairs. And there she stayed. And so did Captain Harry and his crew of thirty-six. England and France had fallen out again, and if a nice boat like that, with thirty-seven potential enemies, walked into a French net, it was hardly likely they would be allowed out again. The cutter was taken, and the thirty-seven men were thrown into prison.

Harry longed to see his family again, and very soon

he saw one of them. John joined him in prison. He, too, had walked into the net!

It was two years before they were liberated, being exchanged for two Frenchmen suffering similar home-sickness in England. When John and Harry got back to Prussia Cove, they found their six brothers and two sisters well but poor. The smuggling business had struck lean days since the two principals had departed. The fact that they now returned without their fine sixty-ton cutter was a further handicap. But the old leadership soon revived fading endeavor, and be-fore very long new boats were built, and Captain Harry was in charge of a lugger with not sixteen guns, but twenty!

The poor man's conscience still worried him, how-ever. He records, with further conscience-pangs, that he "being exposed to more company and sailors of all descriptions, larned to swear at times." This tuition, after about twenty years of smuggling and two in a French prison, arrived somewhat late in the day!

The official attitude toward the Carters was as vari-able as the captain's conscience, and at one time the customs officers were chasing them, at another utiliz-ing them. When an order came from the collector of customs at Penzance to pursue a foreign privateer, the Carters obeyed without any relish for the job, and lost their new twenty-gun lugger in the encounter!

This tragic attempt to serve their country did not assist Captain Harry when, a little later, his smuggling vessel met two man-o'-wars, and was attacked and cap-tured. Captain Harry was severely wounded in the head during the battle, and his account of his escape, after being taken for dead, is so quaintly expressed that it is worth quoting at some length:

> I suppose I might have been there aboute a quarter of an hour, until they had secured my people below, and after found me lying on the deck. One of them said, "Here is one of the poor fellows dead." Another made answer, "Put the man below." He answered again, saying, "What use is it to put a dead man below?" and so past on.
>
> Aboute this time the vessel struck aground, the wind being about east-south-east, very hard, right on the shore. So their I laid very quiet for near the space of two hours, hearing their discourse as they walked by me, the night being very dark on the 30 Jany. 1788.
>
> When some of them saw me lying there, said, "Here lays one the fellows dead," one of them answered as before, "Put him below." Another said, "The man is dead." The commanding officer gave orders for a lantern and candle to be brought, so they took up one of my legs, as I was lying upon my belly; he let it go, and it fell as dead down on the deck. He likewayse put his hand up under my clothes, between my shirt and my skin, and then examined my head, saying, "This man is so warm now as he was two hours back, but his head is all to atoms."
>
> I have thought hundreds of times since what a miracle it was I neither sneezed, coughed nor drew breath that they perceived in all this time, I suppose not less than ten or fifteen minutes.
>
> The water being ebbing, the vessel making a great heel towards the shore, so that in the course of a very little time after, as their two boats were made fast alongside, one of them broke adrift. Immediately there was orders given to man the

other boat, in order to fetch her; so that when I saw them in the state of confusion, their gard broken, I thought it was my time to make my escape; so I crept on my belly on the deck, and got over a large raft just over the mainmast, close by one of the men's heels, as he was standing there handing the trysail. When I got over the lee-side, I thought I should be able to swim on shore in a stroke or two. I took hold of the burtons of the mast, and, as I was lifting myself over the side, I was taken with the cramp in one of my thighs. So then I thought I should be drowned, but still willing to risk it, so that I let myself over the side very easily by a rope into the water, fearing my enemies would hear me, and then let go.

As I was very near the shore, I thought to swim on shore in the course of a stroke or two, as I used to swim so well, but soon found out my mistake. I was sinking almost like a stone, and hauling astarn in deeper water, when I gave up all hopes of life, and began to swallow some water. I found a rope under my breast, so that I had not lost all my senses. I hauled upon it, and soon found one end fast to the side, just where I went overboard, which gave me a little hope of life. So that when I got there, could not tell which was best, to call to the man-of-war's men to take me in, or to stay there and die, for my life and strength were allmoste exhausted; but whilst I was thinking of this, touched bottom with my feet.

Hope then sprung up, and I soon found another rope, leading towards the head of the vessel in shoaler water, so that I veered upon one and hauled upon the other that brought me under the bowsprit, and then at times upon the send of the sea, my feet were allmoste dry. I thought then

I would soon be out of their way. Let go the rope, but as soon as I attempted to run, fell down, and as I fell, looking round aboute me, saw three men standing close by me. I knew they were the man-of-war's men seeing for the boat, so I lyed there quiet for some little time, and then creeped upon my belly I suppose about the distance of fifty yards; and as the ground was scuddy, some flat rock mixt with channels of sand, I saw before me a channel of white sand, and for fear to be seen creeping over it, which would take some time, not knowing there was anything the matter with me, made the second attempt to run, and fell in the same manner as before.

My brother Charles being there, looking out for the vessel desired some Cawsand men to go down to see if they could pick up any of the men, dead or alive, not expecting to see me ever any more, allmoste sure I was ither shot or drowned. One of them saw me fall, ran to my assistance, and, taking hold of me under the arm, says, "Who are you?" So as I thought him to be an enemy, made no answer. He said, "Fear not, I am a friend; come with me." And by that time, forth was two more come, which took me under both arms, and the other pushed me in the back, and so dragged me up to the town. I suppose it might have been the distance of the fifth part of a mile.

My strength was allmoste exhausted; my breath, nay, my life was allmoste gone. They took me into a room where there were seven or eight Cawsand men and my brother Charles, and when he saw me, knew me by my great coat, and cryed with joy, "This is my brother!" So then they immediately slipt off my wet clothes, and one of them pulled off his shirt from off him and put on me, sent for a doctor, and put me to bed.

Well, then, I have thought many a time since what a wonder it was. The bone of my nose cut right in two, nothing but a bit of skin holding it, and two very large cuts in my head, that two or three pieces of my skull worked out afterwards.

How Captain Harry lived to tell the tale was more than a wonder—it was a miracle. And the poor fellow's troubles were not over after that. A reward of three hundred pounds was offered for his capture, and after his injuries had been healed—the doctor who attended him was brought to his house of concealment blindfolded, lest he should try to earn the three hundred pounds!—he spent a year hiding in one house or another. Finally, since the price still remained on his head, the smuggler was himself smuggled to New York, where he had another violent wrestle with his conscience, and became a staunch Methodist.

This ought to be the end of Captain Harry's stormy story. It was not. He returned to Cornwall and preached in the villages where he had smuggled. Then he was warned by someone he describes, mysteriously, as "a great man of this neighborhood," that although he had whitewashed himself with God, he had not done so with the law, and there was talk of his arrest. A final extract from his memoirs will reveal the results of this disturbing information:

> I parted with him, fully determining in my own mind to soon see my dear friends in New York again. So I told my brothers what the news was, and that I was meaning to take the gent's advice. They answered, "If you go to America we shall never see you no more. We are meaning to car on a little trade in Roscoff, in the brandy and gin way, and if you go there you'll be as safe ther as in America; likewayse, we shal pay you your commission, and you car on a little business for yourself, if you please." So, with prayer and supplication I made my request known unto God.

One feels that this strange, rough, simple man went through more than he deserved. In Roscoff he sinned and suffered. He was also thrown into prison again during the French Revolution, expecting every day to be guillotined. It is with relief that we find him back in Cornwall again, four years later, with his mind finally made up to relinquish smuggling forever.

This time he stuck to his resolution. His brothers continued to deal in contraband, but Captain Harry had had his fill of it. He tilled a small farm at the neighboring village of Rinsey, wrote his unique autobiography, enjoyed thirty-four years of peace and godliness, and died at the ripe age of eighty—to ascend, let us hope, to the elusive, beckoning Heaven he ultimately strove to reach.

He was a tall, athletic man,
Well formed to stand in battle's van;
His raven curls appear'd below
The calpac, that conceal'd his brow;
And to that swarthy sun-tann'd face
Did lend a wild peculiar grace.
Such is the man who plough'd the deep—
Whose eye was rarely known to weep.

(This quaint verse forms a part of a poem entitled
"The Smuggler," by "W. L.," published in 1825.)

The Escapes of Jack Rattenbury

JUDGED by his successes, Jack Rattenbury—self-styled "the Rob Roy of the West"—cannot rank as the greatest of all smugglers; but judged by his dogged refusal to succumb to his failures and his limitless capacity for getting out of scrapes, there is probably no smuggler in history to vie with him. He escaped so many times in his adventurous and colorful life that it is a wonder people did not give up trying to catch him!

The son of a Devonshire cobbler, who died before Jack was born in 1778, he was brought up at the little village of Beer with the smell of the sea in his nostrils and the itch of the smuggler beneath his skin. His first experience of the sea was not successful, and it

almost seems as though Fate was offering him a warning which he did not accept. At the age of nine—a
young age, admittedly, to read signs and portents—
his uncle took him on a fishing expedition, and he
celebrated the occasion by losing the rudder. In spite
of this inconvenience the boat got safely back, and
young Jack learned what a rope-end felt like before
he tried to forget his troubles in bed.

In disgrace at Beer, he was apprenticed to a fisherman in Brixham. Here he had further bad luck, for
he was the baby of the apprentices, and he received
very rough treatment. In estimating Jack's character,
we must give him credit for the fact that, while people
used him badly from childhood upward, he did not
use them badly in return. He was a kindhearted
scamp, and the cruelty associated with so many of his
class, and to which he was frequently himself subjected, was alien to his own disposition. Judged by
the standards of his times, he deserved the popularity
he undoubtedly won.

Beer received him back again. It never got rid of
him, and, in truth, it never wanted to. He ended his
days there, as he had begun them, and whenever he
went forth, no matter for how long, he always returned at last like a homing pigeon.

Jack was now thirteen, and his uncle, forgetting
the past, allowed him to join the crew of a privateer.
This delighted Jack's soul, for it spelled both adventure and glory. Unfortunately Jack's privateer, the
Dover, made a bad choice, selected as victim a French
ship with twenty-six guns, and was herself captured.

From a Bordeaux prison Jack made his first escape; but he was sixteen before he had worked his long and tortuous way back to Beer, via America.

Privateering having failed, Jack now decided to try his hand at smuggling, the most popular trade of his district, and he joined a smuggling ship, the *Friends*, under Captain Jarvis. Ironically, when this ship met misfortune, it happened to be on its way to Tenby for a perfectly legitimate cargo of culm. At 4 A.M. on the fatal morning, Jack was awakened and summoned on deck, to learn that a French privateer had forced them to surrender, and that a boat had come alongside to take off the crew. It seemed that Jack could never be on the winning side.

To his surprise, however, he was not ordered to accompany the crew. The French prize-master, who boarded the *Friends* with four sailors, looked him up and down, appeared to decide that this youngster was not dangerous, and told him to remain. He would be another hand to do some work, and there might be plenty before they got the prize back to a French port.

Feeling lonely among strange company, Jack set his wits to work as he watched his companions depart. He had made one escape from a prison. It should be no more difficult to escape from a ship. Docilely, and looking as innocent as he was alleged to be, he hatched his plan.

The prize-master was at the helm, and he was having trouble, for he did not know the coast. Jack offered to assist him. *He* knew the coast, he said, and he also knew the ship. The Frenchman looked dubious, while the Englishman looked cherubic. The weather looked cheerless.

It was the cherubic countenance of the Englishman and the cheerless aspect of the weather that settled the matter. Why waste a willing worker, when it would be so much pleasanter to go below? Telling Jack to steer east-south-east, the prize-master relinquished the helm, and went down to get out of the cold and the wet.

The weather grew worse. A fog rolled up. Shortly after it had rolled away again the prize-master reappeared on deck and gazed, with astonished eyes, at a coastline.

"Where's that?" he demanded.

"Cape La Hogue, sir," answered Jack. "Shall I go ashore and fetch a pilot?"

The Frenchman continued to gaze at the coast line. He was not very happy about it. He let Jack go for a pilot, but he sent three men with him, and when the little boat was near the land an English voice hailed them. The next moment Jack had dived overboard. During the fog he had changed the ship's course from east-south-east to north-east, and this was the doorstep to England.

The enraged men tried to hit his head with their oars, but the head ducked unerringly, and all the oars smacked was water. Fearing capture, the Frenchman gave up, and returned to the ship while Jack swam ashore.

Having saved himself, Jack set about saving his companions. He interviewed the authorities, and the adventure ended with the capture of the privateer.

It was, however, the prelude to another. Expecting thanks from his country, Jack Rattenbury received, instead, the attentions of a press gang. He was forced to join the crew of the *Royal William* at Spithead; but a little thing like that did not worry him. A fortnight in the English Navy was all he could stand, and he escaped again. Then he fell into the hands of the Spaniards—and escaped again! French—English—Spanish—it was all the same to this irrepressible youth.

People began to believe that Jack Rattenbury could escape from the Devil himself!

Back at Beer, he resumed his interrupted career as a smuggler, interspersing this with periods of privateering. He was more successful at the former than at the latter, and he laughed at the customs officials who tried to catch him. There was a certain official, a lieutenant, who particularly disliked being laughed at, and one day he came across Jack in Weymouth town. A stern chase ensued. Jack shook his pursuer off, and at last found sanctuary at an inn, the proprietor of which was one of his customers.

Believing himself safe, he went to bed. At 2 A.M. the innkeeper was awakened by a loud knocking at the inn door. In vain to pretend he had not heard it! The knocking was too loud. He crawled out of bed to admit a visitor who was threatening to smash the door down.

It was, of course, the irate lieutenant. He had traced Rattenbury to the inn, and he was not going to leave the inn until he had found his man. Forcing the innkeeper to lead him to the smuggler's room, he entered it to effect his capture.

The room was empty. The lieutenant searched every corner of it. Then the inn itself was searched, and then the room again. After an hour, the lieutenant swore and gave up. Rattenbury had dissolved into thin air.

When the lieutenant had departed and all was quiet again, Rattenbury wriggled down the chimney. His gift for escape had again proved its infallibility, although in this instance, as his disheveled condition showed, he had only got out of one tight corner by getting into another.

Shortly after this, at the age of twenty-one, he was captured by somebody from whom escape was impossible. He married. But his wife was the exception who proved the rule, and during the years that followed—years in which his smuggling fortunes ebbed and flowed, with rather more ebbing than flowing— his score of escapes steadily mounted.

His next escape was from the revenue tender *Roebuck*. Rattenbury's boat, lined with good kegs, was captured while returning to Beer from Christchurch, and both cargo and crew were transferred to the revenue ship. In the little tussle that had preceded the transference, one of the revenue men had had an argument with his pistol, and the pistol had blown off his arm. The captain sent the poor fellow ashore, and when the boat landed, Rattenbury got out of it too! He had slipped into the boat unobserved and had concealed himself in the bottom.

The exploits of Jack Rattenbury are sometimes difficult to believe, but by far the pleasantest course is to try to believe them, ignoring the fact that many come from his own autobiography. With D'Artagnonlike daring, he hired a boat that same night, returned to the *Roebuck*, rescued his companions, and filled the remaining space of the boat with three of his captured kegs!

Soon after this came an adventure in which his escape was delayed longer than usual. Incidentally, he was the victim of a dirty trick. Returning from Alderney, which he was frequenting now instead of Christchurch, he was sighted by a revenue cutter, the *Duke of York*; realizing that capture was inevitable, he adopted the ruse of sinking his spirit tubs. When the captain of the cutter overhauled him and came on board, there was no contraband to reward the officer for his search.

Unfortunately the captain was a suspicious man, and he knew something of Jack's record. He threatened to detain the smugglers on suspicion, then promised not to carry out his threat if he were told where the kegs were hidden. Jack believed him and revealed the secret. After the captain had regained the tubs from the deep, he broke his word, and kept his prisoners on board with the damning evidence he had cheated out of them.

The *Duke of York* entered Dartmouth harbor. So did Jack Rattenbury, over the ship's side. He swam ashore and dived for a clump of bushes. Two unromantic ladies saw him, and informed on him. He

was caught again, and in due course he was tried at
Dartmouth for his sins.

His fellow smugglers were tried with him, and
the evidence was too damning to be dismissed. The
prisoners were offered the alternatives of:

  (*a*) a fine of one hundred pounds apiece;
  (*b*) service in the Navy;
  (*c*) jail.

They chose jail, for none of them had one hundred
pounds to spare, and most of them had had a taste of
the Navy. But they soon regretted their choice. Their
cell was filthy, and it offered no possible chance of
escape, even to a man of Rattenbury's ingenuity. So
they contrived to exchange the cell for a ship—and a
few days later Jack Rattenbury, having taken advantage of the loosening effects of a naval drinking bout
in which he wisely did not participate, was coolly
walking back to his beloved Beer.

Home once more, fortune favored him for a while,
and he made some successful runs. Fate had to go on
knocking him down, however, if only for the fun of
watching him get up. Captain Hall, of the *Humber*,
was the next instrument. He caught Rattenbury and
a friend redhanded, and in due course they learned at
Falmouth that they were destined for a term of imprisonment in Bodmin jail. On this occasion there
was no option.

Things looked bad. Rattenbury had already proved
that it was easier to escape from a ship than from
jail. Gloom descended on him as he visualized close
prison walls replacing far horizons.

Still, he did not despair. Half his genius was in creating opportunities, the other half in seizing opportunities that created themselves. The opportunity now proved to be the thirstiness of his guards. Humble constables, as well as naval officers, knew how to drink and be merry.

If Black Marias had existed in those times, Bodmin jail would doubtless have provided Rattenbury and his friend with free board and lodging; but the local substitute for the fast Black Maria was the slow post chaise. In this present case there were two post chaises, one for each of the prisoners. The party of six—two prisoners, two constables, and two drivers—set off for the moors and Bodmin.

They stopped at every inn. Rattenbury noted that each time he was rejoined by his constable, that unworthy individual was a little more amiable. The final inn before their destination was the Indian Queen, and as the constables were about to depart for their last drink, Jack begged to be allowed to stretch his cramped legs. . . . Certainly! Why not? Those legs would soon be cramped enough in prison!

So while the constables drank, Jack and his fellow prisoner had a private heart-to-heart with the two drivers. Fortunately the drivers were understanding fellows, and they turned their blind eyes to a fight that ensued when the bibulous constables came out of the inn. They did not even look when the constables, in no condition to offer more than a feeble resistance, were shoved into the chaises. One constable did manage to fire a pistol—but the drivers, apparently, were as deaf as they were blind.

It was the constables who were driven into Bodmin, while Jack Rattenbury and his friend strode homeward across the moors.

And so the story went on. To relate the whole of it in detail would be to risk the monotony of repetition. Rattenbury was caught by Captain Emys, of the *Stork*; handed over to a press gang; thrust on the *Resistance*; escaped to Ireland. He was tracked to a public house.

Set upon by armed soldiers, he picked up a reap-hook, and defended himself in a cellar. His final escape this time was due to a party of friends, who burst into the inn and diverted the soldiers' attention with a spoof story of a wreck. He was caught by Captain Tingle, of the *Catherine*, and escaped with his fellow smugglers in a boat rowed to the brig by the smugglers' wives. Fell on bad times. Found good times again. Survived a tussle with another revenue cutter, though his contraband did not survive with him. Was caught by Captain Cowley, of the *Scourge*, an old enemy. . . .

Had the world turned topsy-turvy? This time Jack Rattenbury did *not* get away! He served a year in Exeter Jail, and Exeter Jail was exceedingly proud of itself for retaining this elusive eel for so long.

But though Jack never lost his spirit, a time comes when the best or worst of us must lose our strength, our health, our quick eyes and our keen judgment. His smuggling continued with varying fortunes and

periodic breaks—one of the breaks, sad to relate, was another eighteen months in prison—but age and gout began to give him more trouble than ever an excise officer had. After resisting his wife's advice to retire, and trying a term of land-smuggling—poor fun, that, when one has the sea in one's veins—he sighed and gave up; and, still in his home village of Beer, gradually drifted from robust action into colorful dreaming.

One thing rejoiced his declining days. His son followed in his father's footsteps. But it is the father, and not the son, who is remembered.

Nanty Ewart, described by a critic as "the best smuggler that Scott, or anyone else, ever drew," attributed his success as captain of the *Jumping Jenny* to his education.

"Pardon me, sir," he once told a young barrister, who was daring enough to question Ewart's word, "my handful of Latin, and small pinch of Greek, were as useless as old junk, to be sure; but my reading, writing, and accompting, stood me in good stead, and brought me forward."

Government V. Smugglers

THE FASCINATING story of England's long war against the smugglers—fascinating to read, but probably described by a large assortment of other adjectives by those who participated—is almost unbelievable in its difficulties and its slow progress. In fact, for many generations it made no substantial progress at all, and as defeats outnumbered victories in larger and larger proportion, the hard-worked, ill-equipped, badly organized men who formed the meager armies of law and order became laughing-stocks.

For some five hundred years the original owlers, confining themselves to wool, had worried authority. The new smugglers, with over a thousand profitable varieties of contraband at their disposal, confined themselves to nothing, and had authority completely non-plused. The smugglers began, of course, before the owlers left off, and many owlers, when wool had lost its financial glamour, deserted the old game for the new.

In the Channel Isles the contrabandists found golden opportunities, and Guernsey became a serious thorn in the governmental side. Being a free port through traditional right, its inhabitants were not slow to realize their peculiar advantages, and the island developed into a very profitable port of call and source of supply for the smuggling community. Much geneva and gin flowed from the north into England *via* Guernsey.

Between 1709 and 1722 the government made four attempts to install a customs officer in the island, but something or other always went wrong. Either the officer was withdrawn—or he vanished!

Even in the heart of London disturbing incidents occurred. Some were reported in the *Gentleman's Magazine*, to the delight of the sensation-mongers. (People reveled in sensation then as now, and it is recorded that women of neurotic or callous temperament visited condemned prisoners to ask for a description of their feelings!) One typical report, in an issue of May, 1733, described how some watchmen of St. Paul's, Covent Garden, and St. Martin's-in-the-Fields came upon a party of nine smugglers between 2 and 3 A.M. The smugglers had a large consignment of "uncustomed" tea. The watchmen, excellent fellows, captured the tea and four of the party, but the other five rascals drew cutlasses and got away.

Four days later the *Gentleman's Magazine* reported a considerably worse affair. The watch stopped two women in Whitecross Street. On their erring heads were baskets containing 117 pounds of tea. After the tea had been taken from them, to be locked up in the watch-house, they affected such penitence that they offered to conduct their captors to a house where further tea was secreted. Two watchmen accompanied them to Bunhill Row. There, conscious that friends were in the vicinity, one of the women suddenly screamed, "Robbers! Robbers!" This was a cue for an attack, and the luckless watchmen found themselves surrounded by smugglers with whips. One of the watchmen was so severely belabored with a whip handle that he was dead in a few hours.

These are merely two cases out of a large number that have been preserved in old records, and we can be sure that many more were never recorded at all. The government had, indeed, a hard nut to crack, and with all its incentives it seemed unable to produce the nutcrackers. The Treasury was being robbed. The country was being terrorized. There were not enough men to fill honest jobs, and struggling farmers often had to pay ruinous wages because they could not get the normal labor they needed. Their men had gone a-smuggling! Well—why not do the same? And many a poor farmer did, to the profit of his pocket if not of his soul.

Who could blame him? When the world is topsy-turvy, individual ideas turn upside down, too.

Even juries became tainted, and a Member of Parliament drew this startling picture in a contemporary debate in the House of Commons:

> In some parts of the maritime counties the whole people are so generally engaged in smuggling that it is impossible to find a jury that will, upon trial, do justice to an officer of the revenue in any case whatever. In those counties where smuggling is become general, the majority of the coroner's inquests always consists of smugglers, so that it has been found by experience that these inquests always bring the officer and his assistants in guilty of murder, even though it be made clearly appear, by the most undoubted testimonies, that the killing happened *de defendendo.*

A big effort, though it bore no fruit, was attempted by England in 1736, which is one of the notable dates in smuggling history. Smuggling was still increasing, and so were public petitions urging the government to do something about it. In France conditions were equally bad; the *Maltotiers,* a body especially organized to suppress smuggling, failed to prevent crimes on a par with those in England. Scotland was likewise in the grip of the octopus, and a terrible incident had just shaken Edinburgh.

This was the Porteous Riot. Nine people were killed, including a Captain Porteous, as a result of the execution of the smuggler Andrew Wilson. Wilson swore to the gallows that his conscience was clean,

THE PORTEOUS RIOT

and although he did admit having somewhat violently helped himself to money from a collecter of the revenue, his dire need seemed to him a sufficient excuse; and there must have been some good in the man, because he had sacrificed his own chance of freedom by jumping on soldiers who were attacking a companion, and keeping them off till the companion got away. It was this unselfish act that had caught popular imagination—though not the imagination of the practical law—and that caused the disastrous riot.

The Convention of Royal Burghs of Scotland met in October of that year and exhorted all good Scotsmen, of whom there remained plenty, to set their faces sternly against both smuggling and smuggled goods. The corporate burghs passed separate resolutions, carrying on the message. And at Westminster the Smuggling Bill, 1736, was passed.

This bill was designed to tighten the already existing laws against smuggling, but it attempted more than it could accomplish.

Instead of getting better, things got worse. In the 1740's smuggling in Great Britain reached its red peak.

Sailors may not care, but the poor excisemen did. They had the most thankless and the most dangerous job in the kingdom. They argued to themselves, "What's the use of making new rules without providing machinery for seeing they're kept? What's the use of increasing penalties if the increase only makes the smugglers more determined not to be caught? Why doesn't the government increase *us*?"

Of course they knew the answer. It was the old, old story: the government couldn't. There were no spare men. The wars had swallowed them.

And so the excisemen were attacked more and more, while the revenue cutters policed the Channel impotently. The Eastbourne affair, the Rye affair, the Hastings affair, the Goudhurst affair, the Poole affair —the list of crimes increased till minds that had been shocked became numb. Inns were entered, and revenue officers were assaulted where they sat. Houses were raided, and suspected informers were dragged out to be killed or tortured. In a clash, ten smugglers were likely to pop up for every one exciseman. The coast-watchers needed eyes behind as well as in front.

The next half-century had little to cheer it. The system of fining counties within whose boundaries unpaid-for crimes were committed had just been introduced, and the Smuggling Bill was altered in 1779 and 1784. Boat-building legislation came along, in the hope of upsetting the smuggling fleets. It became illegal to linger within a certain distance of the coast. No lights could be shown on the shore without official authority. A customhouse, at last, was inaugurated on the island of Guernsey. But the smuggling went on as busily as ever.

The one bright spot, although it did not affect actual smuggling activities, was the breaking up of the dreaded gangs. Possibly it was the Poole affair (described elsewhere) that sounded their death knell. This ghastly tragedy did indeed pierce numb skins, and maybe the bodies of two leaders of the Hawkhurst Gang—Fairall and Kingsmill—had some effect when, after being fitted with chains at a smith's shop in Fetter Lane, they were taken back to their native Kent and hanged, the one on Horsendown Green and the other at Gowdhurstgore. Lacking the bloodthirsty examples of the Hawkhurst men, and sobered by the spectacle of two immortals being eaten by crows, other leaders of other gangs came to the conclusions that gangs weren't quite what they used to be, and that smaller, more easily controlled companies might be preferable. The smuggling gangs, in their most sinister sense, gradually dissolved.

With this one modification, smuggling remained a thriving business and, excepting in the case of the Channel Isles, received no serious check till the conclusion of the war with France.

The setback that saddened the inhabitants of Guernsey was the extension of the smuggling laws to a distance of one hundred leagues from the British coast. Thus, for the first time, the Channel Isles found their style definitely cramped, and the incidents which led to this depressing incident—which the dejected islanders eventually took remarkably well—form one of the most astonishing, and also one of the most amusing, pages in smuggling history.

The Channel Isles, by their position and privileges, played a vital part in the story of smuggling during most of the eighteenth century, and reference has already been made to the earliest attempts to deal with the problem of Guernsey, which, from the smuggling angle, was easily the most important of the islands. Four attempts to establish an official on this island had failed, as we have seen. The fifth attempt, when a customhouse was actually established there in 1767, appeared to have excellent chances of success. The smuggling laws had not then been extended to the hundred-leagues limit, but an order went forth that "no brandies or spirits be imported into or exported from these islands in casks of less than sixty gallons, or in vessels under fifty tons burden," and a schooner of fourteen guns, a cutter, four boats, and forty men, were sent to Guernsey to insure that the order was carried out.

Smugglers favored boats of considerably under fifty tons, since they could more easily evade detection or capture in small, fast vessels; and, of course, tub-carriers could not handle sixty-gallon casks. The usual smuggler's cask was an anker, containing ten gallons, or its smaller brother of four gallons' capacity. This new rule, with the means of enforcing it, looked like being a death blow to the liquor trade.

But the new rule was not enforced! What induced the government's heart to soften? The schooner, the fourteen guns, the cutter, the four boats, the forty men, all melted into a mysterious oblivion, and the islanders breathed again!

Not quite as freely as before, however. Damage had been done. France wanted England to continue its smuggling, and believing that the days of Guernsey were numbered, suddenly provided a substitute. By an edict of the King of France, dated September 3, 1769, an insignificant fishing village in Brittany that no one had heard of but itself was made a free port. Thus Roscoff entered its long and unexpected era of greatness, and became a household word.

Guernsey had prospered. How little Roscoff would prosper in its place! And besides bringing English gold over into France and helping to keep the English smuggling nuisance alive, Roscoff would maintain touch with a class of Englishmen who were often very useful to the nation with which England was at war.

Perhaps this was one reason why the schooner that had arrived at Guernsey so ostentatiously left it so quietly? Strange events and queer attitudes some thirty years later lend color to the theory.

Roscoff had "tasted blood" and remained a free port. Guernsey, however, also continued to prosper after its reprieve, and in spite of its new rival went on making fortunes. So much so that, in 1800, the government decided to send over a commissioner to make a report and issue a warning.

The comedy continued.

The commissioner was one Mr. Stiles. After interviewing the civil authorities of the island, he wrote to the bailiff. His letter was long and impressive. The vital points can be told here at considerably less length. They were that fraudulent trade was being carried on in Guernsey, that it was prejudicial to the interests of England, that it could not go on, that the

Order in Council of 1767 would probably be revived, that fresh regulations would be added, but that in view of the serious difference this would make to Guernsey's business habits, the matter would not be rushed.

The receipt of Mr. Stiles's solemn letter almost sent Guernsey into mourning. While the Royal Courts of Guernsey were working out their reply, the worried inhabitants themselves presented a personal petition. They glimpsed grace beneath the commissioner's solemnity.

The petition was pathetically frank. The petitioners felt alarmed. They frankly said so. Thousands of good people would be ruined. Surely, if the Order in Council of 1767 had not been enforced at the time, it could not suddenly be enforced after thirty-three years? The trade they lost would only go to another country. To an enemy country! Look at Roscoff! Better that Guernsey should make the money, whatever the ethics, than a foe they were fighting! The wealth Guernsey made would revert to the mother country, support funds, and perform other acts necessary to England's greatness.

In short, the petition pointed out that England was bound to be cheated, and that it was much best to be cheated by her own countrymen.

And the reply of the Royal Courts of Guernsey pointed out exactly the same thing, though in far more words.

The island shook under Mr. Stiles's portentous boots as he left it to convey its attitude to Westminster.

Westminster was impressed and thought about the matter for five years. To cheat or not to cheat? That was the question! Whether 'twas nobler in the pocket to suffer. . .

The debate in the House of Lords that eventually decided the fate of Guernsey took place on July 9, 1805. It is doubtful whether any other debate in the holy sanctum of lawmakers has ever so frankly explored the virtues of being swindled. Lord Holland spoke eloquently in favor of the swindlers. If the mischief should be carried on, more or less, it was "better it should be carried on by subjects than by foreigners." His peroration will have to be quoted, since, like the whole debate, it must be unique. After describing the temptations of the smuggler, he wound up:

> All that legislature can do is to compromise with a crime which, whatever laws may be to constitute it a high offence, the mind of man can never conceive as at all equalling in turpitude those acts which are breaches of clear moral virtue.

But Lord Hawkesbury replied for the opposite view with equal eloquence. He did not suggest that the smuggling could be stopped, nor did he suggest that, as between Guernsey and Roscoff, it might not be better for Guernsey to smuggle; but turning his eyes inward, he asked how, if Guernsey's example remained unchecked, it would be possible to check smuggling within England itself.

The Lords kept their heads, though some of them must have been spinning, and the vote was taken. The islanders lost their right to smuggle by nineteen votes to six.

After they had recovered from the shock, they faced the affliction of honesty with surprising fortitude.

From the *Scots Magazine*, dated June, 1778:

"Out of the proceeds of the two seizures of contraband goods from the Isle of Man, made in December last [1777] at the Mull of Galloway and the Clone by Mr. Reid, Inspector General of the Customs, the military who assisted on that occasion have received as follows: the lieutenant, £269, 14s.; the sergeant, £42, 16s. 10d.; corporal, £28 11s. 4d.; each private, £14 5s. 8d."

Eighty Tubs (AFLOAT)

THERE THEY were, eighty of them, standing on the cold stone floor of a Cherbourg cellar. Neat little casks, with broad wooden bands encircling either end, and each cask containing four gallons of the best French brandy. At least, the English smuggler who had raised the money for it in England, and who had now come over to fetch it, hoped it was the best.

"You have tasted it, *m'sieur*," said the French merchant, standing by his side.

"Yes, if this is the same," retorted the smuggler. "Once it wasn't!"

"And so you changed your merchant and came to me," smiled the other. "Believe me, *m'sieur*, I am as honest as yourself. You have the best brandy and the worst weather. The quality of the brandy, indeed, is too good for the numb English palate. What I sell to you does not come from the potato or the beet root."

"I'd slice you if it did," grunted the smuggler. "Twenty shillings! The best price, too! Last trip you let me have 'em for nineteen."

"These are lean times. We have our taxes, too— and *we* pay them!"

"Not if you can get out of it, you don't! Blast this war!"

"You should bless it, not blast it," the Frenchman pointed out. "It provides you with your trade, and diverts your government from the business of stopping it."

"They stopped it last time—"

"But this time will make up for it. Is an English smuggler ever beaten twice running? Attend, *m'sieur*. You complain, yet you pay me one pound for what, in your country, is sold for five. Perhaps you yourself sell it for four. What you sell it at is not my concern. But even that turns the eighty pounds you have so kindly brought me into—for you—three hundred and twenty. This three hundred and twenty pounds can be invested again, and by the same process and the same arithmetic, can be converted into one thousand two hundred and eighty pounds. Take away the number you first thought of—that insignificant little eighty —and you have twelve hundred profit. Where, *m'sieur*, is your excuse for grumbling?"

"Well, I work for my profit," answered the smuggler, "and may hang for it!"

The Cherbourg merchant smiled, and glanced toward the narrow steps that wound down to the cellar.

"If you are going to hang, why not hang for a little more?" he suggested, lowering his voice. "I shall be drinking with one of our naval officers tonight—while you are trying to avoid your own. If I could pass on a little special information to him, my financial position might improve, and I might then be able to let you have the *next* lot for nineteen?"

The English smuggler looked thoughtful.

"Why not this lot?" he inquired.

The French merchant regarded his fingernails.

"The accuracy of the special information would have to be proved," he murmured.

That was a pity.

"I've nothing to tell you," said the smuggler shortly. "Come along, get busy. Let's have the boys in, or we'll lose the tide."

"If that is all you lose, it will be a small matter," replied the Frenchman.

An order was given, and many heavy sea boots, stained and untidy, scrunched down the dark stone steps. The Cherbourg merchant threaded his way through the eighty tubs and opened a small iron door in the wall. In a few minutes, hands used to the job had rolled the eighty tubs through a tunnel to the waterside, and their new, hazardous journey had begun.

The boat waiting there, heaving rather ominously against the harbor wall—the whitecaps out in the bay did not make a pleasant sight—was a twelve-oared

galley. Even without its crop of goods, as the eighty
contraband tubs were called, it had no right to cross
to England, for a recent law forbade any galley carrying more than half a dozen oars to move or lie within
two leagues of the English coast. The port of Bristol
was alone exempt, and this galley was not going to
Bristol. But people who broke one law were quite
ready to break another, and no one had any scruples
as the tubs were brought on board.

The tubs, as well as their contents, spelled fortunes
for somebody. The demand for the liquor created the
demand for the casks that contained it, and the cask-
manufacturers did a roaring trade. Many retired on
their earnings. Others grew rich on letting convenient
cellars and vaults, especially adapted for the storing of
the tubs. By this means alone the smuggling fraternity had permitted one family in the vault-and-cel-
lar business to amass three hundred thousand pounds.
Small wonder that the smuggler achieved with many
both popularity and power.

But none worked for their reward with more skill
and courage than the law-breaking sea-smugglers
themselves.

When the eighty tubs had been stowed on board,
they were no longer visible. You could have roamed
the boat from end to end without coming upon any
sign of them. They had exchanged their dark cellar
for the dark recesses in a double bottom and a false
bow. Here they lay amid the special tackle that would
presently be used for further stages of their journey—
rope slings, drift-lines, and sinking-stones.

"You think you'll make it?" inquired the Cherbourg merchant when all was ready, as he stared northward toward the inclement broken horizon.

"We'll make it," answered the leader of the party confidently. "Our 'gentlemen' are expecting us at dusk."

Evening was the time favored by smugglers for sighting the English coast. Watchers could spot them too clearly in the daylight, but in the grayness of gloaming they could slip homeward like shadows, sometimes mingling with the local fishing craft to disguise their identity and intention.

"It is my experience," sighed the Frenchman, "that in this world we do not always get what we expect."

"You've got your eighty pounds," the smuggler reminded him with a grin.

"And I wish you a good journey so that I may get eighty more," the Cherbourg merchant grinned back. "*Bon voyage, mes amis!* I am very content not to be with you. Are you never seasick, you English?"

Then the galley slipped away from the shore, and the Cherbourg merchant, and the quay on which he stood, and the dirty narrow streets behind him, and the heights behind them, all grew smaller and smaller in the gray blur of a December morning. Grew smaller and smaller till they vanished, and only the eighty tubs, themselves invisible, remained to prove that they had ever been.

The smugglers did not anticipate any trouble at the French end—the French encouraged English smug-

gling, often picking up a bit in more ways than one
—and as they made their way northwestward through
the deep bay they concentrated on the maneuvering
of the boat. They were used to rough seas. Experts
in their work, they were proud of it. They had little
else to be proud of. But the land-smugglers had not
even that, for all they could do—boasted the seamen
—was to carry, slink, hide, run and break heads.

They would certainly have been helpless on this
tossing sea, which was the kind the seamen liked. In
rough weather the coast-watchers were apt to relax
some of their vigilance, while the sea-watchers, the
revenue-cutter men, had quite enough to do to look
after their own safety. A revenue boat was far more
likely to run from a storm, or to succumb to it, than a
vessel manned by a dozen stout smugglers! This was
why winter and bad weather made the best smuggling
combination.

But the present storm proved a terror. The eighty
tubs, rising, falling, swaying, and rolling with the boat,
had a rough time of it. If they possessed souls as well
as spirits, they must have longed to be back in the cool,
quiet cellar, where the floor kept still!

The bay was now well behind. The galley was a
small dot on a vast open sea. The English Channel
only looks narrow on a map.

"*Are* we goin' to make it?" muttered the pessimist
of the party.

"*You* won't, if you don't stop looking like a dead
crow!" retorted the leader.

"That sort o' talk don't get nowhere," grunted the
pessimist. "Wot's the durned wind doin'?"

"Wobblin', like you," answered the leader, staring at the scudding clouds. "Jest the the same," he added practically, "if she comes round much more we'll be into it."

"And if a gale comes and we ship water, then wot?" demanded the pessimist.

"We'll lighten ship and trail," said the leader. "Ay, and we'll trail you at the end of the lot. You're fat enough to float!"

The pessimist laughed with the rest. In a storm it's no good being the odd man out.

It was a storm, too. The gale arrived and blew the exact way they didn't want it. The sea became a mess and tried to get rid of itself into the boat. But still they kept on, making long tracks and maneuvering with uncanny skill. Twelve men and three hundred and twenty gallons of French brandy had to get through the storm somehow. What was more, this crew had a reputation for punctuality, and had only once—on their last trip—slipped up badly. They did not want to spoil a good record.

"I do like the sea, I do!" chanted a seaman.

"Well, don't let anybody know," said another.

"Wot a lot o' trouble fer a little bit o' pleasure," said another, as the tubs rolled beneath the boards, "and gone afore yer knows it!"

They sang a song, but the wind sang louder. Visibility decreased as the salt spray lashed their streaming faces. They laughed derisively. The Navy could have done with them.

Suddenly one pointed.

"Wot's that?"

A ship grew out of a squall of rain away to port, then melted off into a moist mist.

"See us?"

"Dunno!"

"Wot was she?"

"Oi! There's another!"

A second ship materialized in the curtained distance. It came and went like a shadow. The smugglers regarded one another meditatively.

"If they was Frenchies," said one of the men to the leader, "and if they was makin' for England, wot do we do?"

The leader understood the question. There was a story—and he knew it to be true—of a brother in the profession who, accidentally discovering the whereabouts of the French fleet, had risked life, liberty, and cargo by actually seeking a revenue cutter, going alongside, and passing the news on. . . .

"We mind our own business," answered the leader, and then added, for the sake of convenience, "They wasn't Frenchies. Get out the sinking-rope. We ain't far now."

" We ain't goin' to sink the stuff?"

"I wouldn't be too sure!"

Now some of the men busied themselves with the tackle that had been stowed away with the tubs and began preparing for emergency. They worked swiftly and deftly on tackle ingeniously prepared. The tubs were already fitted with their rope slings—this was a part of the merchant's job—and could be quickly threaded onto the sinking-rope which, it now appeared, might have to be used.

They saw no more ships. Dusk set in. As they worked, a long, irregular smudge appeared on the horizon. The Dorset coast developed murkily. Eyes strained and nerves became tense. What sort of a reception were they to get? They never knew for certain.

Apparently they were to get no reception at all. The little shadowy cove that had been selected for their destination, and where the land-smugglers should have been waiting, seemed deserted. No friendly light came across the heaving water from the expected spout-lantern. No sign of movement anywhere. Ominous? Disappointing, anyway. The leader had hoped for a direct landing and a direct run. It would have saved a lot of trouble. The fault in timing was not his.

"Funny thing, ain't it?" he grunted, while the galley drew cautiously toward the bay entrance. The weather had abated slightly. "With the sea and the wind against us we keep our appointments, but land-lubbers can't keep their!"

"Too rough for their boat," suggested one of the men.

"Do they want a duck pond?" retorted the leader. "They could give us a sign, anyhow!"

"P'r'aps someone's blabbed."

Apart from the absence of their working-partners, there was no sign of it.

"Well, we can't land the stuff, and we can't take it back," said the leader, "and we ain't going to be found with it. Got that tackle ready?"

Nothing was going right. The pessimist could have

told them it wouldn't. The night before, as he was leaving a Cherbourg inn, he had seen a cat walking backward. Just as they were ready the weather got bad again, and a sudden gust sent two men flat. They swore at each other. So did the leader.

"We can't sink it in this!" he exclaimed. "Hell!" The boat rocked and nearly sent him flat. "Lighten ship, and tow the damn' stuff!"

More work! The tackle was altered. In a few minutes the eighty tubs were overboard. They bobbed and bounced unhappily, and maybe gave themselves up for lost. They became three hundred and twenty gallons of French brandy playing hide-and-seek in the waves. A sight to make a tippler clasp his head and faint.

But the seamen took it all quite calmly. The stout drift-line to which the tubs were attached was fast to the stern. Before long the tubs achieved sufficient order out of chaos, and the three hundred and twenty gallons of brandy had become a more or less straight line in the galley's wake.

" 'Ow long's this goin' on?" inquired the pessimist.

"Oh, not more'n a 'undred years," answered an optimist.

It went on for half an hour, and during this half-hour the seamen displayed their greatest skill in manipulating the boat and keeping, more or less, their position. Then the wind grew really tired. "You win," it said, and died down.

In comparative peace the final operation was performed. The long line of tubs was hauled in, and the tubs were slung all round the boat. They were transformed from the ship's tail into its necklace. Between the tubs were heavy stones, sufficiently weighty to draw them down to the bottom, and the sinking-rope to which tubs and stones were attached was held in position by slight fastenings from the gunwale and stronger ones at bow and stern.

"All ready?" asked the leader.

"Hey!" gasped one of the men.

In the distance loomed a vessel of unmistakable shape. A revenue cutter.

In an instant the lashings were cut, and as the necklace sank down into the deep, the galley appeared to step out of it. Before the eighty tubs had touched bottom, the boat was veering round from the shore and beginning a new race.

Far from the spot where the cause of many a man's downfall lay waiting for fresh victims beneath the waves, the revenue cutter overhauled the smuggler's galley. It was not quite fair. A second cutter had joined in the chase, and the pessimist had lost his head and his life by jumping overboard.

But no contraband was found on board. The only crime proved against the galley was that its oar capacity exceeded the legal allowance by half a dozen pairs. For that offense it was confiscated and carved by the callous law into three pieces.

The merchant in Cherbourg was very sorry when he heard about it.

"My grandfather's name was Duval; he was a barber and perruquier by trade, and elder of the French Protestant Church at Winchelsea. I was sent to board with his correspondent, a Methodist grocer, at Rye.

"These two kept a fishing-boat, but the fish they caught were many and many a barrel of Nantz brandy, which we landed—never mind where—at a place to us well known. In the innocence of my heart, I—a child—got leave to go out fishing. We used to go out at night and meet ships from the French coast.

"I learned to scuttle a marlingspike, reef a lee-scupper, keelhaul a bowsprit as well as the best of them. . . . I wouldn't go on with the smuggling; being converted by Mr. Wesley, who came to preach to us at Rye—but that is neither here nor there. . . ."

(This astonishing statement was found in the diary of W. M. Thackeray after his death. It was not autobiographical, however—merely a letter written to his publisher sketching the outline of his last work, *Denis Duval*.)

Eighty Tubs (ASHORE)

THE EIGHTY tubs lay on the sea bed among rocks and seaweed. Fishes swam round them, crabs crawled over them. Neither the fishes nor the crustaceans were particularly interested. Strange things came down sometimes, but provided they remained stationary, the sea's inhabitants soon got used to them and accepted them as part of the view.

The tubs, owing to the eighty stones and the large anchor that had accompanied them down, remained stationary.

They had been in the Cherbourg cellar for a few days and in the smugglers' galley for a few hours, but they stayed on the sea bottom for a week. Dark shadows occasionally moved far above them, and on the sixth evening one had behaved rather oddly. It had let down a queer iron contraption, and once the dangling nuisance had nearly caught in the long rope to which all the tubs were attached. It had missed the rope by inches. A few minutes later it had come back, and had tangled itself in mess of seaweed. Then it had suddenly been jerked upward, to be seen no more.

The man who had jerked the iron grapnel upward —in technical parlance it was called a "creep"—was an exciseman; and he swore.

"Thought I had something that time," he muttered disgustedly. "I'm getting tired of this!"

"What about giving up, then?" suggested his companion. It was a cold night. "What about giving up and letting the 'gentlemen' take a hand at the creeping?"

"What do you mean?"

"We can watch 'em, can't we? And if they're more successful than we've been, we can nab 'em on shore."

It was an idea. But the first man was doubtful.

"I don't believe our information right, to begin with," he said. "If you ask me, I don't believe there's any crop here at all!"

"In that case no one will come along, and we'll just lose another night's sleep," the other pointed out. "But if they do come along, and if we take them red-handed, it's promotion for us!"

"They won't come along—we scared 'em away last week."

"Of course we did! More fools us! And they

won't come back till we make a show of finishing.
Do you s'pose they were all collecting here that night
for nothing? We showed ourselves too soon, yes, and
we've shown ourselves too often ever since! Remember that boat that shoved off yesterday full of seaweed——"

"It didn't shove off in this direction!"

"No, when they think they're watched they never
shove off in the direction they end up—you don't want
me to tell you that! If we'd kept out of it there'd have
been tubs under that seaweed when it returned. I tell
you, if anybody knows where the crop lies, they do,
and we must give them the chance."

Logic won the day. The excisemen returned
ashore. And next day, in an alehouse, they sat gloom-
ily while the innkeeper brought them their drinks.

"What's the trouble?" asked the innkeeper.

"Trouble for you," replied one of the excisemen.
The innkeeper's eyebrows went up. "You're going to
lose some customers."

The innkeeper tried not to look worried. He had
some very profitable customers.

"Who?" he demanded.

"Us," answered the excisemen.

Then his companion kicked him under the stained
table, and he shut up. But the innkeeper had heard
enough to want to hear more, and murmuring his
regrets as he put the glasses down, he left them to slip
behind a thin partition. He had heard many secrets
from behind this partition, and the excisemen knew
all about it.

"Silly fool, blabbing like that," said one of the excisemen in a low voice, with a wink.

"What's it matter?" grunted the other, with another wink. "That fellow's all right, and even if he wasn't, the rest will learn soon enough."

"That's no reason for letting 'em know before," came the retort.

"But there's nothing here—we've proved that."

"Of course there's nothing here. Our information was wrong from the start. When we got back a week ago from chasing 'em off, there wasn't a sign in the bay. But we want to keep the scalawags guessing, don't we? Why let 'em know we're quitting. Keep 'em scared!"

While they winked at each other, the innkeeper on the other side of the thin partition winked at himself. Before the morning was through, he had passed his information on to the more profitable customers he had imagined, for a worried moment, he was going to lose. If he charged them less than he charged the excisemen, it was only because they brought him more.

It was a pretty game, prettily played. The excisemen deserved to win it. While the innkeeper was sounding the "All clear," they were completing their plans for their triumph. A mile from the inn they were discussing, with four others—excisemen had to be strictly rationed, and only six could be mustered for the night's job—the best spot to wait in, and deciding on a convenient cave. Many caves were not convenient, but this was one the smugglers did not usually patronize.

At dusk they crept to the cave, armed with muskets. The cave had a dark turn at the end. Poking their heads round to make sure it was empty, they discovered that it was not. A score of thugs leaped out of the blackness, overpowering them before they had time to use their weapons. One of the excisemen was killed, the other five were bound and gagged, and left in the cave to get a wetting from the tide.

The man who had been killed had expected gentler treatment. It was he who had given the show away.

Then the ruffians departed, most of them scattering to spend their share of the two pounds they had earned for the dirty business. They were the dregs of the dregs, lower even than the smugglers, and they had merely been engaged to prepare the way—"so we won't have to soil our hands," one smuggler had ironically informed them. . . .

And now, once more, a dark shadow moved over the eighty tubs that waited patiently at the bottom of the sea while men planned and plotted, lied and cheated, fought and died for them. A lobster, classed lower in the scale of living things than man, was the first to notice anything. An iron claw, descending from nowhere, gave it a crack. Then the claw moved on with a queer dragging movement, disturbed a shoal of fish that became a flash of flying silver, and found something more to its liking. It gripped a rope.

A tub woke from its long sleep and stirred. It tipped upward, sank back, tipped upward again. Its neighbor did the same. The trouble spread as the claw rose slowly and the captured rope tightened in resistance. No rest for the wicked!

As the tubs rose tortuously to resume their interrupted adventure, one suddenly seemed to grow impatient, detached itself from the sinking-rope that was now being converted into a rising rope, and reached the surface ahead of its fellows. It was the one tub that had not slept snugly on the sea bottom, and that had fretted against a bit of rock. In another twenty-four hours it would have "chafed" itself free without assistance from above, and would have ascended to prove the existence of its seventy-nine brethren.

The premature appearance of the winning tub was regarded grimly by experienced eyes from the boat to which it rose.

"Come loose," commented the chief, as the tub was seized and brought on board. He examined the frayed end of the small portion of rope still adhering. "Bit o' luck for us it didn't come up yesterday!"

"Those sea-lubbers made a proper mess of it this time," grunted the second-in-command. "They deserved to be caught!"

The land-smugglers were as fond of denying the virtues of the sea-smugglers as the sea-smugglers were fond of returning the compliment. But the chief was a fair man.

"They had to sink in a hurry," he answered, "and what are *we* boasting about?"

"We've found the stuff—ain't that something?"

"Ay—becos', spite of the hurry, it was dropped in the right spot. Would we have found it without the bearings? We'll talk when we've turned the crop into cash, and meanwhile see *you* don't make a mess of it and earn a whipping and a month. The time to cackle, my lad, is when you've laid your egg!"

"Here they come!" shouted a man deliriously.

"Gawd! Where?" gasped the second-in-command.

"The *tubs*, man, the *tubs*!" snapped the chief. "Keep your head, or I'll tip you over where they've come from!"

At first one by one, then in twos and threes, the tubs popped their heads above water. Dexterously they were shepherded into the fold. Five, ten, fifteen, twenty, thirty, forty . . . eighty. Not a single tub missing. The only casualties, so far, were human ones.

With its valuable cargo, and guided by the spout-lantern for which a week earlier the sea-smugglers had strained their eyes in vain, the boat returned to shore, while the recaptured tubs were quickly severed from their tackle. The little crescent of sand in the small cove presented a strange appearance. In half a dozen circles of light that seemed to accentuate the surrounding dimness, excited figures stood or moved, watching the boat's approach, and as it touched bottom and the torchbearers thronged forward, the light-circles joined in a big, garish blur, half on wet sand and half on the surface of shallow water. The boat was pulled in. Men laughed as the casks began to be unloaded. But a sharp order from the chief controlled dawning delirium, and the unloading continued in whispering silence.

The tubs had been through four operations. They

had been purchased, brought over, sunk, and worked
—the latter term applying to the job of regaining them
from the sea. Now they had to be "run," and there
was as much chance of bungling the fifth operation as
of bungling any. The chief knew this, if some of the
others forgot it, and the first detail was to insure that
his army did not get out of hand.

He made a speech. It was very short and very
much to the point. If the run failed, those responsible
for the failure would be shot. If the run succeeded,

everybody would benefit—by receiving their pay which
they would otherwise go without. The pay for both
porters and batmen—the men who carried the tubs
and the armed guard—was five shillings per head. If
the enemy surprised them and they got into a fight,
the armed guard had damn' well *got* to fight, and
there would be an extra ten shillings for every tub of
brandy saved as an additional inducement. And that
was that.

In a few minutes the procession started. Forty
porters, with two tubs apiece, one slung in front and

one behind, and thirty batmen. With the chief and his second-in-command the complete army numbered seventy-two, but the batmen would be left behind when the horses were reached. They single-filed up the narrow cliff path, and walked two abreast when the path widened into a lane. The tramp of their feet was a warning to all who might hear it. In the night they did not expect to meet anybody. In the daytime respectable people had learned to step to the side of the road, turn their backs, and pretend not to notice. The "gentlemen" ruled the route they traveled.

At the top of the long climb was the inn. During a short halt for breath, the chief took two of the carriers into the inn. The innkeeper, descending from his bedroom in his nightcap, beamed at his visitors. A moment later, however, his face fell.

"Only four?" he muttered.

"Not those unless you have twelve pounds in your fist," replied the smuggler.

"Last time you let me have six!"

"Last time you didn't nearly get us into trouble. Mistakes have to be paid for. Be thankful I'm only charging you three apiece, you dog—I shall be getting four for the rest!"

The innkeeper sighed, paid twelve pounds, and received four tubs. As his visitors left he spat after them, then quickly closed and bolted the door.

The march continued. The procession went through a road with a dozen cottages. No one came out to worry them from the cottages. Only the women were at home.

The farm was the devil of a way off. Why the hell didn't they build farmhouses nearer the coast? A few of the men began to get nervous. The chief was the only one who had a musket. The thugs had gone off with the excisemen's weapons, which in itself was unsettling. Suppose the thugs attacked? Their numbers were smaller, but unless you could surprise a man with a musket, he was worth ten more without. But the greatest fear was of another body of excisemen, reinforced by dragoons. In this game of craft and countercraft, treachery, war without ideals, you never knew where you were—particularly on a dark night like this, when a low wind moaned, and the hedges whispered, and little animals that ought to have been in bed suddenly darted across the road and made you jump. . .

"Wot's that?" cried one of the porters.

The chief, beside him, cuffed him on the ear. All the porter heard after that for a while was a loud singing.

They reached the farmhouse. It showed no light. They passed on to a gate beyond. The gate was opened. They marched through. Beneath a long, low roof were tethered horses.

Now came the second halt. The chief relieved another porter of his two burdens, told the second-in-command to open one, and returned to the farmhouse with the other. He deposited it outside the door. The farmer's wife heard him and shivered. She couldn't see any good in the stuff, anyway. All it did was to make her husband lose the use of his legs. She closed her eyes tight and thought hard of the next life, in her effort to forget this.

The chief returned to his men. The brandy in the opened cask was so good that he had to deliver another lecture. He himself wasn't having any till the end of the journey. Then he'd get drunk for a week.

When the procession was resumed on horseback the army had been almost halved, but there were still seventy-four tubs of brandy. The disbanded batmen had received their pay out of the twelve pounds received from the innkeeper.

Six of the eighty tubs had finished their adventure, and it seemed as though the other seventy-four had also finished theirs. The wooded road was quiet and peaceful, and a horse gives you a pleasant sense of security. These horses were sturdy, too, and could support both men and loads. But suddenly six figures leaped from the trees some twenty yards ahead, and, spanning the road, leveled muskets at the oncoming riders.

The muskets had recently belonged to six excisemen who were now—five bound and gagged and one dead—in a cave.

The chief smuggler did not hesitate. He judged a situation by the men who created it, and if he occasionally made mistakes he made none this time.

"Anyone who turns is dead," he said. "Ride 'em down!"

He set his horse at a gallop. All the others followed suit, irrespective of the will of their riders. The six men wavered. One fired wildly. Then they turned and ran. Three got away unhurt, two had limbs smashed, and one was found next morning by the farmer.

Ten miles away was a town, and the smugglers reached the outskirts without further incident. Dismounting from their horses, they led them quietly into

a back street and halted before an insignificant-looking shed.

A pig opened a small eye and closed it again. It knew what was going to happen, and it wasn't interested. Things got boring after constant repetition. A trap door would be lifted in a corner. A corner the pig had learned by now not to lie in. It got kicked if it did. Then a lot of men would come in, carrying a lot of fat, round, wooden things. The fat, round, wooden things would be put down a hole, and they

would roll away somewhere. Then the trap door
would be closed. Then the displaced straw would be
put back again. Then the men would go. Very dull.
Why stay awake to watch it?

So the pig didn't stay awake. It slept while all this
happened; and while the second-in-command and the

porters rode the horses back to the farm, beating the
cockcrow; and while the chief followed the tubs into
his house and went to bed.

A month later, a man came to see the chief. He
had been four weeks in prison and he had a sore back,
but he was quite cheerful.

"Have you got anything for me?" the visitor asked.

The host smiled, and handed him a slip on which
was written:

Sales				£	s
	74	at	£4 =	296	0
	4	at	£3 =	12	0
	2	at	Nil =	0	0
	80		= £308		0

Expenses

	£	s
Cost of Brandy =	80	0
11 boatmen =	11	0
40 carriers =	10	0
30 batmen =	7	10
Extra help =	2	0
Tom (not worth it) =	3	0
Oddments =	1	10
	£115	0

Now take £115 from £308 = £193 0s
And the half of which sum = £ 96 10s
Less what I paid out more than you = £ 13 0s

And your share is £ 83 10s

Perhaps the excellence of this account was marred by the fact that it made no provision for three dead men.

"Well, where's the £83 10*s*?" inquired the sea-partner.

The land-partner unlocked a drawer and counted it out to him.

Then they drank to each other's honesty in French brandy.

From the *Gentleman's Magazine*, March, 1752:

"An officer of excise at Suffolk, and 2 assistants with fire-arms in pursuit of Rich and Cook, two outlaw'd smugglers, overtaking them in a field near the fens at Mildenhall, received the first fire, after which Rich struck at the officer with an ax, but missed, he then snatched a pistol from one of the pursuers, and firing it, shot out two of his teeth; but receiving two balls in his body, and having his skull fractur'd with blows of the pistol, was taken, but died next morning; Cook escaped."

Snapshots Round the Coast

TO THE average individual who quickly hardens on a term as an easy substitute for personal knowledge or study, the word smuggler conjures up a single picture.

Smith's smuggler may not be identical with Brown's, while Brown's may differ substantially from Robinson's. Smith's may be a fierce fellow in long sea boots, heavy oilskins, and a hood, with a bottle of contraband gin in one hand and a murderous knife in the other; Brown's may wear a short belted coat and a three-cornered hat; Robinson's may be Smee-like and love little children. But whatever picture is adopted by its particular sponsor, it probably remains the same for all smugglers for all time.

This trouble-saving device can be disastrous when applied to matters of real and current importance. Fortunately for our present subject, however, we can do no damage by tarring all smugglers with the same brush; we merely cheat ourselves of an intriguing knowledge of their infinite variety.

There have been generous smugglers and cruel smugglers; heroic smugglers and contemptible smugglers; brave men and cowards; social lions like the amazing Lafitte brothers of Louisiana; queer fish like Jack Rattenbury; humorous rascals like Don Miguel; patriotic adventurers like Harry Paulet; devils like Fairall and Jackson. A complete volume could be written of the life stories of individual smugglers in which no two rascals would appear the same.

And just as individuals vary, so do localities. The Cornish smugglers were different from the "flaskers" of Kent and Sussex, who in their turn differed from the contraband merchants of Norfolk. In America, if you wanted the right men to help you in a little slave-smuggling expedition to the West Coast of Africa, you did not turn to Maine or Long Island; you turned to Cape Cod. You could count on the whalers of New England not being too squeamish for that blackest of all jobs.

The smugglers of the southwest of England seem to have been among the best of the brew, and to have possessed certain qualities which placed them as a class above their fellows. They may not have been the cleverest in the matter of brain, for the smugglers of the southeast were more closely watched, being nearer to the Continent, and were consequently forced to develop more shrewdness and subtlety. Moreover, the men of Kent and Sussex had long tradition behind them, having descended from the original owlers who for centuries had trafficked illegally in wool. But Devonshire and Cornwall folk had their own particular difficulties to contend against—mainly difficulties of distance and a more dangerous coast—and if they did not gain top marks for brain, they gained them for brawn. Their bravery and seamanship were unexcelled.

Frequently they made trips to France across rough winter seas in small open boats, bringing their liquor safely ashore in astonishingly quick time. They were among the last to defy the authorities to any appreciable extent, and kept up their smuggling after the eastern counties had been conquered or tamed. They often enjoyed the game for itself as well as for its profit, and imparted a special atmosphere to the business which lingers strongly in many a Cornish village still. If a film magnate wished to find a perfect setting for a smuggling story, he would not search Kent and Sussex, although Rye would be worth a visit—he would go straight to Cornwall, and would probably end up in Polperro. Not a roof or a door or a stick or a stone would need altering in that strangely picturesque, strangely sinister place. As soon as he descended the hill into the quaint street, where cottages have eyes instead of windows and you feel a spiritual stranger even to the familiar gulls floating above the landlocked harbor, he would sniff triumphantly and cry, "Eureka!"

Polperro turns back the pages, and carries you down its hill into the past. Though of course, even in old-world Polperro, you must be prepared today for the anachronism of the wireless.

This village is typical of Cornwall, for, just as Polperro is a place apart, so Cornishmen were a race apart, and almost remain so today. In smuggling times they stuck to their superstitions, their primitive heroisms, and their sense of humor. With a simple faith that is not universal in this world, they sometimes took glorious risks, and two out many stories may be quoted here to illustrate how heroism and humor could interfere with the certainty of profit.

First, the heroic story. It reads more like a legend than reality. The hero was a smuggler named Peter Trant, who was bringing his lugger back to a hidden Cornish cove one stormy night. A flash of lightning revealed a ship in distress. Trant could not make out the ship's identity, but he made out enough to think about. A mast had gone, the sails were torn from the bolt-ropes, and she was being tossed toward a towering cliff separated from the sea by a short, narrow strip of shingle.

"We've got to get them off," he told his men.

They did not agree. They had had a stiff time themselves, and wanted to land their crop of goods. While the discussion was going on, another flash of lightning illuminated the ship, and now its identity was no longer a matter of doubt. It was a revenue cutter.

"That don't make any difference," insisted Trant.

The men implied, very volubly, that that was all *he* knew! They would follow him pretty well anywhere, but not into the very jaws of the enemy!

"Why, even if we could save 'em, which we can't," they argued, "what'd happen? We'd be took up fer our trouble!"

It was then that Peter Trant committed his first act of mad heroism—the kind of act that was applauded many years later in Adelphi melodrama. He stripped off his Guernsey and dived into the sea! One can almost hear the angels cheering!

Dick Turpin must have had an easier ride to York than Peter Trant had to the revenue cutter. Trant rode over enormous waves, and also under them. What he expected to do when he reached the cutter is not clear, for the ship was doomed, and his men had been perfectly logical in their attitude. Even if they could have got close enough to have taken the excisemen off, the ships must have inevitably have crashed together, and two would have gone down instead of one. Beneath his sturdy exterior Trant must have had a very tender heart, or else a sublime belief in his local knowledge, his nautical skill, and the beneficence of God.

He got to the cutter somehow, but not in time to test his skill. No sooner had he clambered on board than the boat was dashed onto rocks, lifted, and dropped. The rocks had left a great hole in her, and she was a total wreck.

The scared excisemen gave themselves up for lost, but Trant still meant to justify himself. Telling them to follow him, he leaped into the water again and swam and scrambled onto the tiny beach toward which the ship was being tortuously projected. The excisemen followed like frightened ducks. They were so panic-stricken and bewildered—the sudden appearance of the smuggler must have seemed like an hallucination—that they would probably have followed him anywhere. The strip of beach was only a temporary haven, for the rising tide would soon cover it, if the cutter itself did not cover it first.

Trant began climbing the almost sheer cliff. In the shrieking darkness the excisemen climbed after him. Spray splashed up at their feet, and one wave nearly sucked them down before they had ascended beyond the sea's range. They did not ascend far beyond. Hauling themselves onto a narrow shelf, they found they had reached a dead end—and the rising water was climbing up after them.

The tension got on one man's nerves. He lost his head and leaped into the sea to end it. Others might have followed if Trant had not suddenly yelled, making his voice heard above the din of the storm!

"We're safe! Safe! Samphire!"

He had found a tiny sprig in a crevice, but for a few moments the dazed men did not realize its sig-

CAUGHT IN A STORM

nificance. But when Trant added, "The tide won't reach us here," they understood, remembering that samphire never grew below high-water mark.

Encouraged, they waited for dawn, and dawn brought them their last shock. Trant was not among them. While they were mourning the smuggler who had saved their lives, if not in the way he had first intended—they imagined, naturally, that he had slipped into the sea—they suddenly saw Trant's lugger heading away round the coast. Trant was at the helm. In the darkness he had found a means of continuing his climb to the cliff top, had met his fellows, dealt with the crop, and made off, thus sparing the grateful excisemen a pretty problem.

So much for the heroism. Now for the humor. But the two excisemen who, on the point of surprising a run of goods on the Cornish coast, were suddenly seized, bound, and carried to the top of a cliff, were, like Queen Victoria, not amused. They were placed side by side on their stomachs with their heads just over the edge, so they could have a good view of the drop beneath them. They may also have had a view of the goods being landed, but they were given to understand that if they so much as sneezed a gentleman behind them would topple them over.

They thought that day would be their last. They lived, however, to hear much more of that day. When rescued it was found that no gentleman had remained behind them, for there were not enough smugglers to spare, and they could have crawled back into safety, released each other, and given the alarm quite easily.

It need not be imagined that Cornishmen were always successful. A certain Mr. Copping had a quantity of silk which had come the short road from France. One day two excisemen paid an informal call. The Cornishman spied his guests at a distance, and went to greet them with an honest smile while his wife hid the silk. The revenue men did not find the silk, but when Mr. Copping found it he wondered why men married. Mrs. Copping had thought of an excellent hiding place—the oven—but in her flurry she had forgotten that the oven was hot. The silk came out nicely cooked.

Twenty-seven miles from the tip of Cornwall's toe, the Scilly Islanders appear to have been a rougher lot. For many years they depended so entirely upon smuggling that they lost all knowledge of other jobs, and they were particularly unceremonious with customs officials who tried to interfere with the one job they understood!

Passing through Cornwall and Devonshire—Beer, in Devon, was the birthplace of the famous smuggler Jack Rattenbury whose story is told elsewhere in this volume—we come to the central southern counties, Dorset and Hampshire. Smuggling was prolific on both coasts, and if Dorset has not provided any special smuggling characteristics of its own, it has given us a most illuminating example of the legal confusion that existed there. In fact the Dorset magistrates seem quite frequently to have been beaten in their attempt to work through the confusion, and they were not helped by the fact that witnesses and juries were generally smugglers themselves with not the slightest ethical interest in the law.

In July, 1833, a magisterial order was issued in Dorset to discontinue the practice of trying several smugglers together for the same offense. The reason for this was that the magistrates were frequently floored by some technical objection which resulted in the acquittal of all the prisoners. By trying them singly, however, they had a chance of profiting by experience, and of applying that experience to the men who were tried last.

The disadvantage to the prisoner of being tried last soon became obvious, since by the end of the day the magistrates had learned how to avoid being tripped up. How the magistrates improved on their sagacity, showing they could be quite as smart when pressed as the smugglers themselves, is suggested in the following instruction issued a few months later:

A case having occurred in which, out of five smugglers brought before the Dorsetshire magistrates, the most notorious of the party, who was tried first, escaped conviction owing to some technical flaw in the proceedings, it is ordered that in future the first one to be tried should be one whose conviction is of least consequence.

A sort of "knock-up" before the actual match!

Hampshire, nearest of the south-coast counties to Sussex and Kent, came within their sinister shadow, and what can be said of Hampshire can be said of Sussex and Kent on a larger scale. Countless atrocities were committed within its boundaries, and the Poole Customhouse affair with its terrible sequel will ever remain one of the blackest blots in the history of the free-traders. The Hampshire men were well provided with smuggling nooks and corners, and the useful Isle of Wight was only about seventy miles from the French coast.

Probably the Hampshire lawbreakers were among the most relentless in the land. Centuries earlier their ancestors had molested the foreign traders who wended their way from Southampton to Winchester. Now they molested their own kind.

But who, at this date, can enter completely into the smuggler's mind, and understand all the queer impulses that moved him as he lost his moral anchorage? What, for instance, is to be our verdict on the famous Hampshire smuggler, Johnson, who adopted strange attitudes and performed deeds both black and white?

In the dawn of the nineteenth century Johnson was a sore problem to the authorities. He outwitted them

continually. But when, on the Continent, Napoleon
offered him a large sum if he would pilot a French
fleet to the English coast, he is reported to have answered, "I am a smuggler, but a true lover of my
country, and no traitor!" Limelight, please, and applause from the gallery! And the applause goes on,
for after being imprisoned at Flushing for his patriotism, he escaped, got back to England, offered his services to the Navy, and was given a job on a revenue
cutter, the *Fox*. Here, having "turned honest," he
molested both his old pals, the smugglers, and the
French, and there is no doubt whatever that he showed
enormous physical pluck in the operations.

Yet what are we to think when we learn that later
on he was prepared to offer the fruits of his ingenious
brain to the very man—Napoleon—to whom he had
declared his staunch love of England? Johnson was
one of the first men to try to invent a practicable submarine. In the 1890 edition of *Whitaker's Almanack*,
in an article on "Submarine Warfare" which shows
that men's brains were busy with the problem long
before 1914, occurs this passage:

> The remarkable invention of the celebrated
> smuggler, Johnson, had for its object the carrying
> off of the ex-Emperor Napoleon from St. Helena
> to the United States, and had it succeeded the
> history of Europe would have been changed. The
> boat was 100 feet long, with masts and sails that
> could be doused and stowed away handily when
> diving became necessary. Johnson was to have
> been rewarded munificently after the exile's es-
> cape, besides receiving £40,000 on the day when

his boat was ready for sea. The death of Napoleon, however, put an end to the scheme.

Perhaps Johnson did not think much of his boat, and imagined it might cause the death of Napoleon in any case. Perhaps he wanted to earn £40,000 for the job of ridding the world of one of its gravest dangers! He might have considered it an ironic trick to receive his pay from the man he meant to drown in his new toy. This is an improbable theory, but improbability gets a mind with a twist in it.

So much has already been said about Sussex and Kent, the hotbeds of smuggling, that little can be added to enlarge on the characteristics of their free-trading population. Before the advent of the coast guards and the "Triple Cordon," and especially during the period of the gangs, one of their chief traits was an impudent brutality. Later, the brutality became converted into devilish cunning. In a sense, the Sussex and Kent free-traders had no particular features, since they embraced them all.

Closeness to the Continent was not a smuggling essential. It was merely a smuggling convenience, otherwise the practice would have been confined to the counties of Kent and Sussex. Just as the game extended to the extreme limit of Cornwall and then round beyond Lundy Island—for some reason Bristol appears to have been fairly well-behaved, since that port was exempt from some of the anti-smuggling laws—so it ran up the east coast of England, and by no means stopped when it reached the Tweed. Scotland has many a smuggling yarn to tell.

From Essex to Norfolk smuggling was rife, and East Anglia has its full share of free-trade memories. To those who possess a complex for these things, the Green Man, at Bradwell Quay, is well worth a visit. While drinking liquor honestly come by, you can also imbibe a strong atmosphere of the days when the liquor served there was not so honestly come by. You may also chance on an ancient native who, even without liquid encouragement (though that would help) will spin you smuggling stories beyond belief. And you will be under no obligation whatever to believe them, though the majority will be true.

Mersea, in the words of an old salt more picturesque than polite, "was fuller smugglers 'n dogs be o' fleas." However unjust this statement may be to dogs, you have only to stand on the quaint Mersea shore with its muddy inlets and creeks to believe it. Mersea was a smugglers' Mecca, though today it is as honest as the rest of the world (if that is saying anything), and secretes only oysters.

All the way up to Norfolk the pleasure-steamers pass smuggling territory. Brightlingsea, St. Osyth, the Naze, Felixstowe, Aldeburgh, Lowestoft, Yarmouth—every sea town where lawless brains congregated and every river that flowed eastward into the ocean—had its worried excisemen watching for the slippery free-trader. Norfolk itself was riddled with contraband and secret storehouses, and with smugglers of the most unscrupulous kind.

While there is nothing special to say about the characteristics of most of the eastern counties, Norfolk had a very evil reputation for cruelty. But you would never think it when moving among its amiable blue-jerseyed fishermen of today.

In Hunstanton churchyard is an epitaph which is as pathetic as it is illiterate. The inscription records a story typical of the times:

> In Memory of William Webb, late of the 15th Lt. D'ns, who was shot from his horse by a party of Smugglers on the 26 of Sepr. 1784.
>
> I am not dead but sleepeth here
> And when the trumpet Sound I will appear
> Four balls thro' me Pearced there way
> Hard it was I'd no time to pray
>
> This stone that here You Do See
> My Comrades erected for the Sake of Me.

Will you hear of the Cruel Coppinger?
He came from a foreign kind;
He was brought to us by the salt water,
He'll be carried away by the wind.

OLD CORNISH SONG

The Curse of Coppinger

I F A dramatist were combing smuggling history
for a subject for a play, he would probably pause
at the story of Daniel Coppinger. He might even
think that the historians had fallen to the lure of
drama in preserving that story, and had embellished
it without strict insistence on the truth. There is a disconcerting neatness of construction, particularly in the
opening and the final curtain, while the incidents of
Coppinger's life contain just that mixture of thrills and
humor, humanity and inhumanity, usually considered
necessary to satisfy all tastes.

The play would open, inevitably, with a prologue
showing the dark shore in North Cornwall on which
Coppinger was washed up—for, to the credit of Cornwall, this brute of a smuggler was not a native of that

county. He was not a native of England at all, being a Dane who was shipwrecked on England's coast, but he lived in England long enough to stamp his curse upon it, and to leave an indelible, black memory behind him.

The night was one of the stormiest for years, and the beach was lined with people, many of whom deserved the unpleasant gift the sea was bringing them; for the majority were wreckers, quite ready to assist in the doom of any unfortunate ship that looked like coming to grief. That, in fact, was what the wreckers had left their fires for. One man's wreck was another man's profit!

But some of the folk had less unworthy motives, and Dinah Hamlyn, watching from her horse, had been drawn to the spot for the mere sensation of the occasion. Before she rode home again, she received more sensation than she had anticipated.

For a while it seemed as though the watchers were going to get nothing from their trouble. Then a ship developed in the stormy gloom. It looked unreal as it smudged vaguely into view, and the unreality was increased by its strange rig. A foreigner, obviously. But, what was more important, a foreigner in distress. The ship was heaving and tossing perilously as it headed for the shore.

As the misty outlines grew more distinct, details were made out. The behavior of the ship had told that it was a wreck, but now frightened figures were revealed, clinging to the rigging and hanging onto solid objects that had not been washed away, while breaking waves sent spray high above them, and water slid or poured down the slopes of the deck. But one figure—the giant at the wheel—showed a different emotion. From this man came curses instead of moans, and fierce anger instead of terror. As was proved later, he had neither reverence for an occasion nor sense of humor with which to meet it. Man, God or the Devil received the same ferocious indignation when attempting to thwart him.

The ship's condition was hopeless. Its canvas was in shreds. It heaved on its impossible journey to the shore till it struck the inevitable rock. Then, while men scurried and tumbled about like frenzied rabbits, their shrieks inseparable from the shrieks of the wind, the giant left the wheel, threw off his coat, revealing by this action a massive chest, ran to the ship's side, poised himself, and dived into the water.

The sight of the giant had already filled the watchers with superstitious awe. The next moment added to their superstition. As though shoved backward by the impetus of the dive, the ship reversed its course, to drift, sinking, away from the coast.

The sea that night claimed many victims, but it did not claim the giant. He had been given up for lost when his huge form suddenly emerged among the breakers. Somehow or other he had plowed his way through the maelstrom, and somehow or other he now clambered out of the water onto the beach. No one helped him out. This person wasn't human! No one approached him while he lay for a few moments, panting back to life. The crowd seemed to realize instinctively that here was a man who needed no other man's help, because he helped himself. And his next action proved it.

He rose, dripping, from the sand. He looked round the watching throng. He was cold, and he wanted something to cover himself with. He chose the red cloak of an old woman. Seizing it from her, he wrapped it round his nakedness, and then glared at the company as though to say:

"Any objections?"

None was offered.

Next, his eyes fell on Dinah Hamlyn and her horse. If he appreciated both, it was the horse he needed at the moment. Plowing his way through the crowd as he had plowed through the sea, he reached the horse, jumped up behind the girl, and shouted.

Dinah made no more protest than the old woman had made. Like her, she was too astonished. The horse, equally astonished, bolted, and did not stop until it reached its stable.

The words shouted by the man had been foreign, though the horse had appeared to understand them. Now, leaving the horse, he strode into Dinah's house and addressed her parents in broken English. He informed them that his name was Coppinger and that he was a Dane—and a minute later he had commandeered a room, toppled exhausted to the floor, and fallen asleep.

The fact that Daniel Coppinger did these things, and that they were accepted without question, provides the keynote to his character. Men obeyed him instinctively because he filled them with instinctive fear.

As he began, so he went on. He slept till next day, and it never occurred to the Hamlyns to disturb their self-invited guest. They probably thought him better asleep than awake, and that thought was accentuated when, just as the family were about to sit down to their morning meal, Coppinger strode into the room, dressed in Mr. Hamlyn's best suit, and coolly took his place at the head of the table!

The strange meal proceeded in silence. The silence was due partly to the facts that Coppinger knew very few words of English and that mere polite conversation was unsuitable to the occasion. Dinah studied the guest quietly, her mother speculatively, and her father amusedly. Mr. Hamlyn seems to have been a simple-minded fellow who reinforced his mildness with a sense of humor, but it is doubtful whether even he submitted to Coppinger's behavor entirely to enjoy a good joke. Both he and his wife may have wondered how the joke was likely to end, and whether they could help that end, by patience and tact, to become a profitable one. Their daughter Dinah was still eligible, and a man of Coppinger's physique would be useful about the farm. The one disturbing factor was the Dane's enormous appetite!

And while the Hamlyns speculated, so did Coppinger. He had lost his ship, but he himself had found a harbor, and his shrewd mind quickly summed up the harbor's possibilities. He had a way with women, and he liked them well enough if they understood

their place. It should be easy, if he decided, to make
Dinah interested in him. He had a way, also, with
men, as we have seen, and he could size up a simpleton when he met one. If Hamlyn had turned him
out of the house, there would have been a row, which
would have ended one way or another. The fact that
he had not done so formed a sound basis for further
impudences. A man who lets you take his place at
table might one day let you rule his farm. And when
Hamlyn died, it would be useful to be his son-in-law.

No one will ever know how much of the future
was actually divined over that first silent meal; but
all these things came to pass. Controlling the cruelest
side of his nature, and developing the farmer's friend-
liness, Coppinger made the ensuing days pleasant
enough; and, being a handsome giant, he very soon
had Dinah under his spell.

He married her—her father died—and Daniel
Coppinger took over the management of the farm, all
according to plan. Incidentally, the Dane also took
over the late farmer's fortune, though Mrs. Hamlyn
wisely hid what belonged to her.

And now his real nature came out, and Dinah's
short spell of timid happiness was over. Even while
the mother and daughter were grieving over Hamlyn's
death, Coppinger commenced his thoughtless treatment of his wife, began spending her money, and invited the worst characters in the neighborhood to assist
in the spending. The quiet farm was awakened into
rude noise and laughter. Wild parties became the
order of the night. And when all the money was

spent, Coppinger did not have to look far to find a means of making more. He formed his cronies into a smuggling gang, and terrorized the country.

It was now that he earned the name of "Cruel Coppinger," and no man in the West Country deserved his title more.

Not far from the farm was a precipitous cliff some three hundred feet high called Steeple Brink. He made this his headquarters. At the base of the cliff was a cave that could be reached only from the sea until Coppinger added a second approach via a cable-ladder, extending from the top of the cliff to the bottom. Much contraband came up this ladder, and Coppinger grew rich again.

Of the many stories that were told of him, three may be briefly related to give a cue to the rest.

Coppinger's most famous smuggling ship was the *Black Prince,* and his methods at sea were so unscrupulous that revenue cutters usually gave him a wide berth. When the cutters had the misfortune to sight the smuggling ship, it was probably the latter that did the chasing! But one day a cutter, commanded by an officer of unusual bravery, decided that Coppinger should not have it all his own way, and made for the ill-famed ship.

The officer expected the *Black Prince* to stay and fight. To his surprise, the ship fled. "Aha! We've got that fellow on the run at last!" cried the officer, and began the chase with comprehensible pride. Even if Coppinger were not caught, the officer could return with the boast that the archsmuggler had been scared!

It looked, however, as though the *Black Prince* were really going to be captured at last, and as she changed her course, wriggling to get free, the revenue cutter stuck grimly to her heels. Presently the two ships approached a spot known as Gull Rock. The channel leading to it was a deathtrap to anyone who did not know it. Coppinger knew it, but the revenue officer did not, and only the *Black Prince* got through. The cutter ended on the rocks, and went down with every soul on board.

The second story did not end in loss of life, but in its way it is no less grim, and it reflects Coppinger in the most despicable light. It has been mentioned that Mrs. Hamlyn hid her money. Coppinger discovered the fact, but not the hiding place, and when he had run through his wife's fortune he tackled his mother-in-law. For a long while he was unsuccessful. Dinah had grown to dread her husband by now—her love had been short-lived—but old Mrs. Hamlyn still retained some spirit, and doggedly refused to give her secret away.

Then Coppinger sank to the lowest depths of his nature. He did not use physical violence on Mrs. Hamlyn—that might have been of no avail—but he threatened to use it on Dinah. After binding the girl to a bedpost, he invited her mother to watch him whip her with a "sea-cat." "But, of course," he remarked ironically, "if you tell me where your money is, there will be no need for Dinah to suffer." He brandished the whip, and Mrs. Hamlyn gave in. She brought him her little fortune, and it went the way of the rest.

A whip figures in the final story. In this case it was used on the local parson, who had possessed the temerity to pay Coppinger a call and tell him what he thought of him. Then, adding insult to injury, Coppinger invited the smarting parson to dine with him, and forced him to eat rook-pie, a dish the reverend gentleman loathed.

"And that's the end of *him*," the Dane decided.

But he was wrong. The parson, in return for his meal at the farm, invited Coppinger to a meal at the parsonage. Coppinger laughed and accepted, and when a pie came on, made every rude joke he could think of at his host's expense. He had to admit, though, that the pie was good, even though its exact nature evaded him.

He discovered the nature on his way home, when
he happened to put his hand in his pocket. He drew
out the skin of a cat!

And so to the epilogue. For Daniel Coppinger was
not destined to poison Cornwall forever. A time came
when the revenue men began to close in upon him,
and his period of successes was waning.

The end came, so declare our dramatic historians,
on a night of storm similar to that in which he had
arrived. Once more the wreckers lined the shore, and
once more their eyes beheld strange sights. One sight
was Coppinger, on Gull Rock—the rock to which he
had drawn the revenue cutter to its doom. Another
sight was the *Black Prince,* tossing a little way off.
A rocket went off from the rock. The *Black Prince*
boomed a salvo in reply. Then, fighting its way
through the seething waters, a small boat went from
the ship to the rock, collected the solitary figure standing there, and took him back to the ship. As though
to insist that Coppinger should fade out in some act
of cruelty, the historians give us a final picture of his
gleaming cutlass slashing a rower who dropped an oar
just as the *Black Prince* was reached. A few moments

later the ship was vanishing toward an invisible horizon, bearing the Danish giant away forever.

Like Lafitte, Don Sebastian and many another, Daniel Coppinger drifted out of history as mysteri- ously as he had entered it.

Aul' Johnnie was a pawky loon;
A pawky loon, I trow, was he;
At smuggling on the Solway coast,
Bune ithers aye he bore the gree.

Ilk creek and cove he weel did ken,
Frae Airds roun' to the Hangit Man,
An' when a lugger was to meet,
Aul' Johnnie sure was in the van.

Outwitted were the gaugers a',
Aul' Johnnie Gir' was aye their match,
For ne'er wi' a' their plans sae sly,
The dodgin' smuggler did they catch.
          SIR WALTER SCOTT

                    Galloway Gleanings

Highland Spirits

THE HISTORY of smuggling in Scotland
has its own special flavor, and that flavor is
whisky. Long before the American bootlegger became a household word, the Scottish illicit spirit-
distiller was hard at the game, and while brandy came
from the French coast and the Channel Isles, whisky
was produced prolifically in the isolation of countless
Highland glens and mountain rifts. The two essentials
in selecting the spot were that it should be as inaccessible as possible, and that there should be running
water.

The preventive men of the North had their difficulties, as had their brethren in the South. For a
long while in the whisky-smuggling history of Scotland the lawbreakers outnumbered the officials, and
struck terror into many a lonely heart. The system

in vogue included the establishment of what were known as Preventive Stations and Preventive Rides. The stations were manned, as a rule, by an officer and two men—sometimes only one man—and for six nights in every fortnight this meager army slept at the station to keep a watch on the more important localities. Then, in the other eight days, they embarked on the "rides," generally undertaken singly, into more remote parts where trouble was expected to be less, but sometimes turned out to be more.

One solitary exciseman, for instance, who came upon a cart laden with whisky kegs in an isolated district, got more than he had bargained for. The cart was in the charge of two burly rascals. The exciseman challenged them, informed them they were his prisoners, and attempted to justify the information by capturing them and the cart singlehanded. The smugglers were astounded at the man's audacity. What! one paltry exciseman against two Highland champions of whisky? The daft idea almost weakened a body with laughter! But when they had got over their astonishment, they grabbed the unfortunate exciseman, tied his wrists to his knees, trussed him up like a fowl, and stuck him in the middle of the lane.

When he pointed out that he would probably be run over in the dark, they conceded the point, lifted him up, and dropped him by the roadside.

The excisemen frequently got the worst of it through being outnumbered or outwitted by the enemy, but an incident at an inn at Dalnashaugh brought them defeat from an unexpected quarter. It occurred on the traditional dark and stormy night, when a postmaster of Kingussie stopped at the inn on his way home from Aberlour.

He was tired and wet, and a couple of hours of rest, food, drink, and smiles from a pretty maid were just what he needed to put him right for the remainder of his journey. All went satisfactorily till half a dozen new visitors turned up. These were gaugers—excisemen—making a halt on their way to Badenoch. Their business was to raid some illicit stills; but, like the postmaster, they wanted a little consolation before completing their far less enviable journey.

Their consolation ended that of the postmaster, who, to his dismay, was relegated to the kitchen so that the new guests could have his parlor. He, a postmaster, was treated as less distinguished than common excisemen! He would soon have put them in their places, and shown the pretty maid that a postmaster was not to be insulted—if there had not been quite so many of them! As it was, he had to get his own back by other means.

He still had the companionship of the maid when she was not attending to the wants of the gaugers, but even her smiles could not soothe the wound to his dignity; and as she appeared from the parlor laden with six pairs of damp boots, and placed them by the fire to dry, he hatched his plan.

Biding his time, he watched for the maid's first yawn, then proposed that she go to bed. She agreed that she was tired. Probably she was tired of the postmaster, whose mood had deteriorated. Saying good night, she left him with the boots.

A few moments later the boots were enjoying a new experience. Outside, in the rain, they had had a cold bath. Now they had a hot one, in a large pot of boiling water which the maid had left over the fire!

Then this exceedingly naughty postmaster, completing the bad work of transferring his personal injury to the community, went out into the moonlight, rode his pony to Badenoch instead of Kingussie, and warned the smugglers that a party of gaugers would be visiting them shortly—as soon, indeed, as they had found and put on their boots.

It took the gaugers less time to find the boiled boots than to put them on. A preliminary bath of boiling water does not ease the process. When, at last, the indignant men reached Badenoch, they found only empty bothies for all their trouble.

The famous poet, Robert Burns, was himself an exciseman for a few years before his death. The work does not seem to have helped that human and tragic figure to overcome his own difficulties, and perhaps the job of Inspector of Liquor Customs is not the wisest for one whose personal liquor customs needed inspection. It is said that the riotous company into which Burns was thrown contributed to his early death, and he did not hesitate, in some of his verses, to round on the very work in which he was assisting. Coming from an exciseman, for instance, there is a quaint irony in his lines:

"Thae curst horse-leeches o' the' Excise
Wha' mak' the whisky stells their prize."

Nevertheless, he performed at least one notable and heroic deed that figures in smuggling history to the poetic exciseman's credit.

This occurred in 1792. A smuggling brig was in the Solway, and looked like presenting some difficulty to the little band of excisemen and dragoons gathered on shore to circumvent it. Burns was of the party, and he waded into the water, sword in hand, and made for the boat. He endured risks from quicksand as well as from the smugglers, but he reached the brig, was the first of the party to board her, and arrested the crew, taking the boat afterward to Dumfries to be sold.

Burns was a man of many virtues tripped up by his vices. With better luck—if his loves and his lands had prospered, and if his literature had received its just commercial reward—he might have been a happier man, though he would not have left a more lasting memory. Perhaps it is not surprising that smugglers and others have failed in their obligations to a system which, often enough, seems to have done so little for them. Discouraged by poverty and his fight against too heavy odds, Burns decided when he was twenty-six to emigrate to Jamaica, and in order to raise money for this trip he published a book of his verses. The verses brought him fame, so he went to Edinburgh instead of Jamaica, but unfortunately the fame was greater than the profit. The book brought him £20. A single copy of this volume today is worth a small fortune.

The name of Robert Burns wanders vaguely in and out of smuggling history. The same cannot be said of the names of George Smith, Shaw, and Yawkins. Yawkins was a Dutchman possessing more than Dutch courage. When his smuggling lugger, the *Black Prince,* was seen approaching from the horizon or materializing shoreward out of a mist, brave men (we are assured) shook in their shoes. Incredible stories are told of him. Here is one.

He was unloading contraband near Kirkcudbright, at the Manxman's Lake, when he saw two revenue cutters approaching from different points. One, the *Pigmy,* was drawing near from the Isles of Fleet, while the other, the *Dwarf,* was between the point of Raeberry and the Muckle Ron. Was Yawkins worried? Not in the least! He weighed anchor, hoisted a cask as his flag, and sailed so close between the two ships that he tossed his hat into one and his wig into the other. These were all the excisemen got out of him, saving a chase in which they were hopelessly beaten.

The chase was commemorated in the following verse:

The mountain-like billows that washing the shore,
Where Raeberry's turrets stood frowning of yore;
The King's men were foiled as she left the isle bay;
With a cask at her maintop in boasting array,
The sails of the cutter spread fast in the wind,
But the *bukker* of Yawkins soon left them behind.

One may conceive, perhaps, that the unexpected and original missiles which landed on the cutters' decks rendered the crews temporarily impotent through astonishment.

Yawkins was the original of the character of Dirk Hatteraick in Walter Scott's novel *Guy Mannering*.

The tales of George Smith are easier to credit, and have a more authentic sound to them. Smith, in his early days, was a whisky-smuggler, so when he turned honest and became manager of the Glenlivet Distillery, he knew all about both sides of the game. He knew, also, that his position was delicate, and that the smugglers would do all they could to smash honest distilling in the glen. For his safety he was presented with a pair of hair-trigger pistols by the Laird of Aberlour, and he always carried the weapons in his belt.

Smith's distillery, of which he became manager in 1824, produced some hundred gallons of liquor per week. During the next two years, three other distilleries opened in the glen, but the threats of the smugglers soon closed them again, and Smith continued his monopoly of legal liquor traffic. The most ruthless of the whisky-smugglers was one Shaw. He owned a shebeen in the wilds of Mar, on the Shea Water. His tavern was a hotbed of iniquity, and only the bravest exciseman would appear in the vicinity alone. Shaw, a giant of enormous strength, would stick at nothing in an extremity.

One wild night Shaw returned to his tavern to find a surprise. He had left the place in the sole charge of his wife, and while she had been there alone no less a person than George Smith had called to shelter from the storm. Most people would have preferred the storm to Shaw's kitchen, but Smith was the exception that proved the rule. Mrs. Shaw, indeed, had been far more anxious for her guest's safety than

the guest himself, and her anxiety was accentuated by
the fact that before Shaw had married her, there had
been a strong probability that George Smith would.
Since he refused to be intimidated by the situation, she
had allowed him to remain, and had locked him in a
bedroom.

Shaw, like many another ruthless man, had a regard for such courage as he himself possessed. He
had returned to his tavern with a band of smugglers,
mostly drunk, who considered this a good moment
to finish Smith off, but Shaw thought otherwise.
Death seemed to him a poor return for his guest's
courageous impertinence, and he decided, instead,
merely to frighten the life out of him.

He led the drunken party up the stairs to the bedroom. Smith opened his eyes to see a murderous band
gathered round his pillow. The light of a torch increased their evil aspect, and the hiccoughs which
punctuated the preliminary silence did not add to the
sweetness of the occasion. Nor did the gleaming
butcher's knife in the great hands of Shaw.

Breaking the uneasy silence, Shaw advanced the
knife toward Smith, and said, "This gully, mon, iss
for your powels!"

The reply was swift and effective. Beneath the
bedclothes Smith was gripping his two faithful pistols.
In a flash the pistols came sweeping out of the bedclothes, and one of them was presented full into Shaw's
startled face. Smith promised to blow the face to bits
if the rest of the company did not immediately depart, and to prove that he was a man of his word—
though this really needed no proof—he extended his

other arm with his other pistol, and, taking advantage
of the fact that his bed was by the fireplace, fired up
the chimney.

The result was a deafening cloudburst of soot. The
drunken smugglers fled. The man with the butcher's
knife, however, remained to roar with laughter at the
man with the gun; and the rest of the night passed in
peace.

In spite of the heroic ending of this story, Shaw
was not the popular hero-smuggler of fiction. The
majority of his dealings were totally lacking in nobility
or humor.

Although whisky is the commodity most closely associated with Scottish smuggling, and has therefore been dealt with here at some length, other contraband found its way into Scotland, as elsewhere, and Scottish housewives thanked the smugglers for reducing their general household expenses.

An amusing tale is told of one Scottish housewife—Maggie McConnell—who reflected the gratitude appropriate to the age in her own particular way. She made friendly approaches to a customs officer who was guarding some seized goods, threw her arms round him, bowled him over, flung her apron over his eyes, and sat upon him till the smugglers had regained their belongings.

A popular form of contraband in Scotland was salt, the duty on which at the beginning of the nineteenth century was exceedingly high, and another story in which a woman came to the rescue—this time with cunning, not with avoirdupois—is related of a perplexed salt-smuggler of Stoneykirk.

One evening he arrived back at his farm in a state of agitation. He had with him two bags of salt, but he had after him a larger number of excisemen, and as he began searching the house to find a hiding place for his contraband, he had already given it up in his mind as lost. But his wife was not going to let a good thing go, and she gave her daughter orders to undress and get to bed as fast as she knew how. "Wha' for?" gasped the girl. She learned when her mother tucked her up in bed with two bags of salt for company.

When the excisemen arrived, they demanded to search the house. No objections were raised, though they were asked to be as quiet as they could, owing to the illness of the daughter of the house. To this they sympathetically and gallantly agreed, and they conducted a tiptoe investigation. When every room had been stripped but the girl's bedroom, they regretted that they would have to strip that, too. Entering softly, and still on their toes, they proceeded to do so. But there is a limit even to official zeal, and of course the one place they did not strip was the bed. Their job was to catch smugglers. Possibly they feared that, if they went too close to the bed, they might catch something else.

One final dip in the rich bag of Scottish tales—and the last, as it should, shall be best.

One sad day, the owner of a still was visited by excisemen and caught redhanded. The excisemen departed with his only keg of whisky.

Apparently the excisemen were not used to success, for their triumph appears to have gone to their heads. At an inn where they put up for the night they made exceeding merry in an upper room. Placing the captured keg in the middle of the floor, they sang and danced round it, while one of them sat on it to keep it from disappearing. They had captured a keg, and no one was going to take it from them!

No one did. When they were about to continue their journey next morning, the keg was still there. But nothing was in it. Some friends of the smuggler, marking the spot on the floor where the keg had stood, descended to the room immediately below, drilled a hole in the ceiling, placed an empty keg under the hole—*et voilà!*

The De'il cam' fiddling thro' the town,
    And danc'd awa' wi' the exciseman;
And ilka wife cry'd, "Auld Mahoun,
    I wish you luck o' your prize, man."

We'll mak' our maut and brew our drink,
    We'll dance, and sing, and rejoice, man:
And monie thanks to the muckle black De'il,
    That danc'd awa' wi' the exciseman.

There's threesome reels, and foursome reels,
    There's hornpipes and strathspeys, man:
But the ae best dance e'er cam' to our lan',
    Was—the De'ils's awa' wi' the exciseman.

ROBERT BURNS

Hide-and-Seek

T H E   Q U E E R fascination of smuggling is nowhere more apparent than in the endless games
of hide-and-seek which it involves. Even today there
are people who will smuggle "merely for the fun of
it." These modern, airy, respectable lawbreakers are
apt to forget that the fun can be expensive if it is not
successful, and that either they or their country will
have to pay in the end for their amusement.

But today's fun cannot compare with that of yesterday, when smugglers had to hide themselves as well
as their goods. While it is true that, in his heyday,
the most impudent smuggler performed much of his
work in the open, there was always more to be done
in the dark, and he would have been helpless without
his hides and "private places" and secret retreats.

The novelist, G. P. R. James, who studied the subject for his romance *The Smuggler*, gives an illuminat-

ing picture of old-time conditions in the following passage:

Each public-house was supported by smugglers, and gave them in return every facility possible. Scarcely a house but had its place of concealment, which would accommodate either kegs, or bales, or human beings, as the case might be; and many streets in seaport towns had private passages from one house to another, so that the gentleman inquired for by the officers at No. 1 was often walking quietly out of No. 20, while they were searching for him in vain. The back of one street had always excellent means of communication with the front of another, and the gardens gave exit to the country with as little delay as possible.

Very many of these hides still exist, and it is as hard to find some of them now as it was in the days of their use. The search for others leads to disillusionment. Let us suppose, for instance, that you discover yourself in the dim cellar of some medieval mansion, gazing at a closed archway and creating romantic pictures of its past. Surely those bricks are cheating your eyes of a tunnel? You study the archway, and leave the cellar to try to work out the alleged tunnel's course. In a musty room above you find some brickwork that appears to be filling some erstwhile slot. "Another way in?" you wonder.

You continue your investigations. You leave the house and search for the tunnel's exit. You believe you find it in a low portion of the outside wall, among a tangle of undergrowth and a dried river bed. You go home in triumph to report.

And then some inconsiderate, heartless historian throws cold water on your enthusiasm. Actually, drainage water. You have merely been exploring a medieval sewer or water conduit!

In the days before modern sanitation was dreamed of, the majority of houses had no sanitary systems at all, but the largest and most important residences were dignified by deep wide drains. Running as a rule immediately under the house, these drains were stone or brick-lined, and vaulted. They received the sewage, bearing it to river or moat, and their generous dimensions were due to the periodic necessity of sending a servant down into them to sweep them out.

In the numberless cases where ancient houses have survived their original drainage systems, these passages have generally been bricked up.

Similarly, you may come upon an ingenious hiding place behind a paneled wall, or beyond the false back of a cupboard or even in a tiny room halfway up a wide chimney—first hole to the right! The majority of these will be interesting enough, but only the minority will possess any smuggling history. In the days of Queen Elizabeth, when Catholics in England went through their thinnest time, no Jesuit priests were allowed in the country, and it was the job of the pursuivants to catch them. Despite the enormous risks involved, Roman Catholic priests remained in, or returned to, England in large numbers in order to keep their torch burning, and it was for the concealment of these that most of the hides you will come across today were constructed. The priests were in worse plight, when caught, than were the later smugglers, for they had fewer friends, and their inevitable penalty was death.

Of course, many priests' hides were subsequently converted to the smugglers' use, while it may be claimed that the original priests who hid in them, having been smuggled into the country, constituted smuggled goods.

One of the most interesting of hides, described by Mr. Granville Squires in his book *Secret Hiding Places*, was at Kinson Church, near Bournemouth. There was two repositories here, one being up in the belfry. If the parson of the period had profited by his own teachings, he would have insured that only bats joined the bell in the belfry; but while the bats flew round, the barrels climbed up, and the places where the barrels bumped against the coping stones, and where the hauling-ropes wore into the crenelations of the tower, may be seen to this day as evidence against him!

The second place of concealment was a tomb to

the left of the vine-covered porch. A corner of the long, flat top-slab is now broken off, probably due to the fact that bars were used by the smugglers to raise the slab when requiring the space beneath for their goods. It seems that only two people were ever buried below the stone, and there was plenty of room for more. The smugglers utilized the extra space for other purposes.

There is little doubt that here, as in many other churchyards which for a period became smugglers' sanctuaries, the local clergyman knew what was going on. He cannot have been as blind as the bats that swooped round that barrel-stocked belfry! But it is too easy, after a long lapse of time that wipes out details, to criticize on general grounds, when the details might prove largely extenuating. Hypocritical some of the country parsons may have been. They would not be the first black sheep to wear white garments. But we need not assume that religion was, as a rule, a willing smugglers' accomplice, protecting with a contented heart the folk it preached against. Clergymen in those troublous times were often placed in an impossible position, and many may have argued, like politicians, that in a crisis idealism must be scrapped for expediency.

The soldier runs away to fight again. The preacher closes his eyes to preach again!

Climbers in Scotland may investigate a famous spot known as "Dirk Hatteraick's Cave." They will need both enthusiasm and nerve for the job, since the hole is high up in a cliff, and to reach its narrow, bush-covered entrance they will have to scramble over an outer ledge, and then, taking a breath, drop about a dozen feet onto the gravel floor. Once inside, however, they will be rewarded for their trouble. In the fairly large interior they will find holes in the walls where the smuggler kept his kegs, places for weapons, and an excellent cellar. Also a chamber, with traces of furniture, which is believed to have been a primitive bedroom.

Dirk Hatteraick's ghost stands by your side in the dimness of the cave, listening with you to the familiar sounds of the wind through the cliff-bushes, or the boom of the sea below.

Another famous cave, on Rathan Island, is described by Crockett in *The Raiders:*

Of a truth they were rather pleasant places as caves go. Of one of them especially I was fond, for not only had it a sea entrance wide and high, which made it safe to enter by boat, but after one had penetrated a long way through passages and halls, mounting ever upward, he came to a space of clear yellow sand, from which there was an opening to the sea, for all the world like the window in a house high up above the doorway.

The cave entrance beneath was, as it were, the door of the house, and within it the tides for ever surged and swirled, while the window at the top looked out to sea midway down the cliff, where not even the samphire gatherer could come nor yet the sea eagle build her nest.

This was the Great Rathan Cave.

Scottish folk were particularly clever in the art of concealment, and they were assisted by the rugged configuration of the coast. They called all their hides "brandy-holes," whether or not brandy were hidden in them, for liquor was the commonest commodity the Highland smugglers dealt in. Their favorite method was to bring the contraband into a rocky bay, and to utilize a cave-tunnel for the secret conveyance of the goods inland. The tunnel usually emerged under a farmhouse, communicating with the cellar through a false wall of rock. If the tunnel and the house refused to coincide, some other device had to be arranged. One tunnel ended inside a haystack!

Another underground passage, in the smuggling district of Cummertrees, ran between a cellar and a peat-stack. The value of this was emphasized early one morning when the farmer's wife looked out of her window and saw a couple of excisemen approaching. Warning her husband, who was still in bed, she rushed down to the cellar to remove certain embarrassing contents that had been stowed away there. By the time the excisemen arrived, the cellar was empty, the said contents having been transferred to the peat-stack; and all the excisemen got for their trouble was a scolding for their suspicions.

Smugglers' wives often came to the rescue of their menfolk, and it was the wife of a south-coast miller who once saved a number of kegs by her speed and ingenuity. The kegs were at the bottom of the mill-pond, held down by heavy weights. Normally the muddy surface concealed them, and many a riding officer had passed the pool unconscious of the valuable secrets it contained. They searched the house, but never thought of the water. On this day, however, while the miller was conducting them over his premises, he suddenly caught sight of the pond and beheld a disturbing sight. His kegs in the pond were poking their noses above the surface!

Once more it was the woman to the rescue. Whispering the bad news to his wife, he urged her to do something while he prolonged the search inside the house. Her quick wit divined both the cause of the trouble and the cure for it. The water in the pond had dropped to this alarming level because no fresh water was coming into it; so she slipped out of the house, hastened upstream, and released the flow. The remedy very nearly proved self-destructive, for the sound of the racing stream fell upon the riding officers' ears, but when they turned their heads the rising water had just performed its work, and the kegs were once more covered.

This was a case in which still waters did not run quite deep enough, but another story, incidentally providing the origin of a curious term, tells of waters that ran very deep indeed.

Some Wiltshire excisemen came one evening upon a party of men raking a river bed with long rods. It was an unusual kind of recreation, and the officers paused to ask for an explanation.

"You see that cheese down there?" replied one of the men. "We be goin' to get it out."

He pointed to the reflection of the moon. The officers stared, then split their sides with laughter. They were looking for smugglers, not village idiots, but here was something for their trouble—a good story! They left the men to their unique fishing, and told the story to all they met. In due course it passed to other counties, till the expression "Moon-rakers" became indelibly associated with Wiltshire country bumpkins. As a name, the "Wiltshire moon-rakers" has lived to this day, and there is even a Wiltshire dart-club existing under that title.

But loudly as the excisemen laughed, it was the moon-rakers themselves who laughed last. The "moon" for which they had been raking at the bottom of the river was sundry tubs of contraband spirits!

A priest living in Dauphiné was so carried away by the exploits of Louis Mandrin that, after the hero's sixth campaign, he inserted in the Register, among baptisms, marriages, and deaths, the following lines:

Brave Mandrin!
Que ne fais-tu rendre bon compte
Brave Mandrin!
A tous ces maltotiers de vin
De sel, de tabac, qu'ils n'ont honte
De voler pauvre, riche et comte?
Brave Mandrin!

(The explanation of which unpriestlike sentiment will be found in the following pages.)

Mandrin the Magnificent

IN ORDER to understand the story of Louis Mandrin, France's smuggler-hero, and to see him clearly against the background of his times, it is necessary to know how smuggling arose in France and what particular kinds of problems it presented. Smuggling may be a universal art, but in each country the artists have always had their special inspiration and characteristics.

The method by which French taxes were imposed and collected in the eighteenth century was outrageously unjust. The taxes, called *les deniers du roi*, were due to the King, but the trouble and uncertainty of collecting them were so tedious to a monarch who was generally very busy enjoying himself that he farmed them out for a fixed sum to a number of gentlemen known as *les fermiers-généreaux*. These farmers-general, numbering about forty, grew fat while the poor taxpayers very ruthlessly exploited grew thin. They were in the secure position of owing allegiance to only one person—their ruler—who did not care a rap what they did so long as he himself was not troubled, and who permitted them to increase old taxes or to invent new ones much as they liked.

The French monarchs could, of course, claim precedents for their behavior. The *fermiers-généreaux* were similar to the *publicani* of republican Rome. This, however, did not excuse the callous system.

Everything taxable appears to have been taxed at one time or another, in one province or another. A list for 1730, for instance, includes among its items salt, tobacco, wine, candles, farm goods, even farm-leases, all manufactures, transport, sales, and business deals. It was a grace that one could sneeze and cough without expense. The fact that each province had its own frontier added to the complexities of the situation. If an Englishman imagines what it would be like to pay duty on articles conveyed from one county to another, or an American what it would be like to declare articles passing from state to state, he will get some idea of what commercial life was like at this period in France.

Of all the French taxes, none was hated more than *la gabelle*, the tax on salt. The *gabelle* was not imposed in every province, but where it was imposed the price of salt became preposterous, growing to twenty-five times the cost of the commodity today. You had to buy your salt—if you could afford it—at one of the King's warehouses; and the general restrictions, designed to preserve the profits for the farmers-general, read more like fantastic invention than actual historical fact.

Here are some of them. You were not allowed to use sea water for any purpose other than bathing or shipping. If you permitted your cow to wander to a salt stream and slake its thirst there, the offense would cost you three hundred livres (about fifteen pounds), plus the cow. It was a crime to put a grain of salt in a turbot before selling it. If you ran out of salt, you were not allowed to make good the deficiency by any private process.

A case is quoted by Taine in his book, *Ancien Régime*, of two sisters who found themselves saltless in the middle of the week, and who did not want to wait for a fresh supply till Saturday, this being the only day on which they could purchase it from the warehouse. They hit upon the idea of boiling down the remains of some pickling brine. Some unkind person informed on them, and the few grams of salt they obtained cost them forty-eight livres. The fine would have been heavier if influential friends had not pleaded on their behalf!

The salt comedy developed. It was not comic at the time, but in retrospect one cannot avoid seeing its humor. Salt grew so prohibitive in price that a time

came when poor people stopped buying it. Since the
vast majority of folk in France were poor, the warehouse lost their customers, and the farmers-general had
to do something about it. What they did was more
amazingly impudent than anything they had done before. They procured legislation by which every man,
woman and child had to buy seven livres' worth of
salt every year!

The amount was small, but multiplied by the population it grew into a very nice total. The annual sum
this law brought in was fifty-four million livres. Having, so to speak, tasted salt again, the public decided
that it must have more, only the balance would have
to bought at a reasonable figure. The salt-smuggler
arose, and solved the difficulty.

The smuggler's job was perfectly simple. Salt was
not taxed in all the provinces—such as Brittany—and
all he had to do was to convey salt from an untaxed
province into a taxed one. His ingenuity was quite
equal to the occasion.

The farmers-general scratched their heads and
found another brain wave. A fresh law was passed,
forbidding people in the non-salt provinces to buy
more than fourteen livres' worth of salt per annum.
This produced the strange anomaly that whereas in
some provinces the housewife was forbidden to buy
more than a certain amount of salt, in other provinces
she was forbidden to buy less than a certain amount.

Of course, this did not stop the smugglers, for by
now their appetites had been thoroughly whetted and
nothing would hold them back. From salt they turned

to silk, cloth, cotton, muslin, calico, tobacco, tree-bark, watches, jewels and prayer books, obtaining supplies from Savoy—then an independent state—and Switzerland, and using Dauphiné as the door to France. As the smugglers increased, the farmers-general augmented the number of their agents. These agents, acting on the instructions of their employers, became a terror throughout the land; and in this connection an interesting comparison may be made of conditions in France and England. In England it was the smuggling gangs that terrorized the country. In France, the smuggling gangs were well organized and well disciplined, and it was the agents of the farmers-general who made folk shiver in their shoes. The popularity of the smuggling gangs is indicated in the following lines, sung by the people of Dauphiné:

> *Alerte! alerte! mon joli coursier,*
> *Vite, vite dans la montagne,*
> *Emporte le contrebandier!*

The French *contrebandiers* certainly ran grave risks. An edict issued in 1726 set forth many severe penalties. For smuggling silk, lace and other articles of this category, a fine of two hundred livres was imposed for the first offense, and six years in the galleys for the second. In certain circumstances the punishments were increased. For instance, to be caught with horses augmented the fine to three hundred livres, and the period in the galleys to nine years. A smuggler who could not pay the fine was flogged, had burning iron applied to his shoulders, and was sent to the gal-

leys. In case of women and girls, the penalty was
flogging. But this was for unarmed smugglers. A
smuggler caught carrying arms was executed. If he
used his arms, he was broken on the wheel.

The tobacco or salt-smuggler was regarded as too
heinous for any fine. He was sent to the galleys or
the gallows. Women had the *fleur de lys* added to
to their flogging.

The French preventive men were called *gâpians,*
and there were about twenty-four thousand of them.
The majority were in Dauphiné, which by its geographical position was the province best suited to the
smuggler's needs; and it was in Dauphiné, therefore,
that the ruthless *gâpians* incited the deepest indignation. No part of the French map was more appropriate for the birthplace of Louis Mandrin, who was
destined to strike a blow for the downtrodden people
unparalleled in smuggling history.

Mandrin was born at St.-Etienne-de-Saint-Geoirs,
near Grenoble, in 1725. He was the oldest of eight
children, and when his father died, in 1742, he followed in his footsteps and became a merchant. He
was a typical Frenchman, always talking, laughing,
drinking, smoking, or loving, and his energy was
boundless.

For five years after his father's death he lived the
life of an ordinary citizen. Then the War of the
Austrian Succession came along, and with it an opportunity for his first big gamble. He turned his attention to mules, which were needed by the French army
of Provence for the tricky journeys across the Alps into

Italy, and by procuring and organizing supplies he began to make money. But unfortunately for the mule trade, the war did not last, and October 18, 1748, ended Mandrin's temporary prosperity when peace was concluded at Aix-la-Chapelle.

Mandrin found himself poor again. As a smuggler, however, he had "tasted blood" and he endeavored to build his fortunes up again by smuggling tobacco. He began in a small way, and it did not get him far. On the contrary, the smuggling of the Mandrins produced a tragedy. Louis's brother, Pierre, was caught by the farmers-general, and was tortured and hanged.

It was this event that changed the course of Mandrin's life by giving him a burning purpose from which he never deviated. He swore that he would devote all his energies to paying the farmers-general back, with interest, and although it was his brother's death that fired the spark, he found plenty of additional fuel to bring the spark to a flame. It is difficult to judge Mandrin's character completely from the records that have been left of him. All the incidents of his life are not to his credit. But there must have been a strong streak of idealism in his nature, and his methods were the methods of his times. He saw in the *gabelle* an oppressor not only of his brother, but of the downtrodden people with whom he was surrounded. He had a genuine desire to liberate them.

For a while he contented himself by increasing his tobacco-smuggling, and harrying the authorities that way. Then, after a scrap with the militia, during which he escaped unhurt, he was outlawed and sentenced to the most dreaded torture of the times—to be broken on the wheel. Since he was still at large, the farmers-general had to content themselves by carrying out the sentence on his effigy! This somewhat strange method of soothing indignant justice—about as unsatisfactory, one would imagine, as hitting a pillow when one is cross—did not trouble Louis Mandrin, although his outlawry meant that he had to look around for new headquarters.

He found them in Savoy and Switzerland, joining a big band of smugglers under one Jean Bélissard. Belissard must have been as remarkable in his way as Mandrin was in his, for after a short while he recognized the fact that the new recruit was a better leader than himself, stepped down, and gave Mandrin the reins.

Now Mandrin had his chance. He changed from a Rabelais to a Napoleon. While he retained his ebullient spirit, he added the solidarity necessary to effective leadership; and he showed vision, as well. He did not spoil his chance by undue haste. He confined his activities to the smuggling business for which the gang had been created until he had increased his numbers with new recruits. And when, at last, he felt his army strong enough, he told the men of his ultimate purpose. This, in effect, is what he said:

"All this while the farmers-general have been trying to break us. They have not been able to do so. We have prospered and expanded. Now are we going to turn the tables, and break the farmers-general. We

shall not do so by stealth, but by open warfare. Are
you all with me?"

They were, to a man. Or, perhaps one should say,
to a Mandrin, for so they called themselves. The
Mandrins set about preparing for the coming struggle.
They were ready by the end of 1753. In 1754 they had
entered France, and, with startling audacity, had begun their little war.

Historians divide the conflicts of that astonishing
year into six campaigns, the first of which lasted from
January 2 to April 5. It opened with a swift attack.
The Mandrins swooped into Chartreuse, made for the
King's warehouse, put the guards to flight, rifled the
place, and swooped away again.

The whole thing was so rapid that the people of
Chartreuse hardly knew it had begun before it was
over!

Then the smuggler-warriors continued their march
into France, raising necessary money on the way by
disposing of the contraband they had brought with
them. They found ready purchasers. The sympathy
of the populace was on their side, and their daring
increased their popularity.

Naturally, the enemy did not take that first defeat
sitting down. Mandrin received information that the
gâpians were preparing to launch a surprise attack.
But it was Mandrin who delivered the surprise. Selecting some of his best men, he went to meet the
gâpians, and scored his second victory.

Brigadier Dutriet heard of the *gâpians'* defeat. His
lip curled, and he declared that if he had been with

the *gâpians,* it would have been a very different story. Mandrin heard of the boast, and in the middle of the night called upon the brigadier to discuss the matter with him. The form of Mandrin's argument was to drag the scared brigadier out of bed and to threaten to kill him. Fortunately for Dutriet, he had a wife, whose pleadings averted bloodshed.

In this third victory there were no casualties, unless we reckon the brigadier's pride. That was put out of action for many a night to come.

The victorious march continued. The smugglers went through Dauphiné, selling their contraband, firing on *gâpians* at sight, and liberating prisoners. They did not liberate every prisoner, showing a nice sense of selection. Smugglers and deserters were given their liberty; the rest had to stay where they were.

In Mandrin's birthplace, St.-Etienne-de-Saint-Geoirs, he made a complete clearance of the *gâpians,* and laughed derisively when he heard of the threats of their employers, the *fermiers-généreaux.* "*Les gâpians? Ah, je m'en fiche!*" he exclaimed.

It was not through fear of them that he turned his men and marched back to Switzerland. For the moment he had done enough, though on the way home he paid one more call. This was at the château of a wealthy man. Here, without asking, he and his men took refreshment, and several other things as well, leaving in exchange the remainder of their contraband. Probably the unwilling host preferred what he had lost to the silk and muslin he had gained, but at least Mandrin could continue his boast that he was an honest swindler, and never descended to common thieving!

So ended the first campaign.

Mandrin spent the next two months reorganizing his army. Recruits flocked in, till the army swelled to a couple of thousand. Most of the new Mandrins were army deserters, some of whom he had himself liberated, but he showed the same discrimination in his army as he had shown at the prisons. He would have no traffic with what he described as "real criminals." (Smugglers and deserters were in quite a different category.) This may have been due to his dislike of genuine ruffians, but probably he was also actuated by sagacity. He needed discipline in his army, and men who would not obey rules were of no use to him.

All his men received regular pay—ten louis on enlisting, thirty sous per day in times of peace, and six livres in times of war.

In the second campaign, which lasted five weeks, the smugglers turned up at Grenoble. Here they had the best of an encounter with the authorities, and brazenly sold their goods in the streets. These operations were repeated at Millau, into which his army trooped on June 22nd, and where he occupied the market place. There in a single day he sold goods to the value of six thousand livres, and in every case the purchaser got a good bargain.

The farmers-general began to grow desperate. Their *gâpians* were no match for the Mandrins, who were growing bolder and bolder, and carrying on their illicit trade with impunity. It was an ironical position, for the smuggler-soldiers were financing themselves by committing the very offense for which they should have been apprehended.

The farmers-general tried something new. They made it a crime to deal with the smugglers. But the boomerang came back and smote them. Mandrin countered by forcing the farmers-general themselves to be his customers! His first call, when entering a town, was at the King's warehouse, to the officials of which he said, "I must have customers, and you are interfering with my old ones. Now, here is some good tobacco—much better than yours, and also much cheaper. I sell it cheap, you know, because I don't pay any duty on it. You will purchase some, won't you?"

The warehouseman always obliged, since the request was accompanied by an impressive display of force.

So *that* was no good!

A rich landowner took a hand. He offered three

thousand livres for Louis Mandrin's head. Mandrin came upon a poster announcing the offer, and went straight to the landowner's castle. "Here is my head," he said, "though I am afraid I cannot leave it with you." Then he claimed the prize money, and the landowner, fearing for his own head, paid up.

When the smugglers had got rid of all their contraband, they ended their second campaign and marched back to their Swiss headquarters. There was one grim incident on the return journey. Louis Mandrin met the man who had been instrumental in his brother's capture. It was a meeting he had long desired and dreamed of. . . .

The third and fourth campaigns were repetitions of the first and second, with variations. The Mandrins grew stronger and stronger, and the *gâpians* grew weaker and weaker. Then, at last, the farmers-general did what they ought to have done before. They enlisted the assistance of the French Regular Army. The *argoulets,* commanded by La Morlière, stepped in to try to succeed where the *gâpians* had failed, and when Mandrin started his fifth campaign he found himself up against a stiffer proposition.

The introduction of the *argoulets* in France can be compared with the introduction of the dragoons in England, when the latter were called in to assist the harassed riding officers.

The third and fourth campaigns had taken place during the three summer months. Now, at the beginning of October, the Mandrins marched into France again. It was a different France. He was fighting the country now, not merely one aspect of it. But he still had his victories, though they cost him more; went successfully through Bourg; and at Le Pûy, in the middle of the month, overcame the stiffest resistance he had so far encountered.

The *argoulets,* knowing that Mandrin would march straight to the house of the farmers-general's local official (for Mandrin was still insisting that these embarrassed gentlemen should be his first customers), preceded him there, and fortified the residence. When the smugglers arrived and opened their attack, the *argoulets* fired from their concealed positions, picking them off. Mandrin withdrew his men, having lost the first bout.

The second attack was a direct one on the door. The smugglers rushed it, dodging bullets, and then belabored the door with a heavy hammer. The door held firm, however, and the situation got too hot. They had to retire again. Round two to the *argoulets.*

Then Mandrin decided that, ordinary methods having failed, he must trying something extraordinary. Detaching fifteen good climbers from his army, he sent them up to the roof of an adjoining house. It was a perilous ascent, for the climbers had to risk firing as well as falling, but they reached the roof, and then poured into the official residence through windows.

The *argoulets* were now caught. The only escape from the menace above was the street, and the Mandrins were waiting there grimly for fugitives. So the

THE MANDRINS AT LE PÛY

argoulets yielded, and Mandrin chalked up another success under his name, albeit a costly one.

Having rifled the house and "paid" in kind, the Mandrins returned to Switzerland. In their fifth campaign they had covered 750 miles, amassed considerable wealth, defeated the new menace, and immeasurably increased their popularity. True, they had lost more men than in any ·previous campaign, but new recruits more than made up for the deficiency.

Then, after a lapse of six weeks, the last campaign of the year began on December 15, and the Mandrins marched forth to meet a strengthened foe.

It is surprising that the authorities faced the reality of the situation so slowly. They could not claim lack of experience, for this was the sixth tussle within twelve months, and in all the previous five they had been thwarted. The cavalry, under Lieutenant-Colonel Fischer, now sent to reinforce the *argoulets,* might have come upon the scene with advantage many months previously.

But, even so, Mandrin was not dismayed. His successes, his popularity, and his own increasing strength, were making him more confident than ever, and he meant to go on until he had liberated France, or been stopped in the process by a bullet.

While Fischer waited for him on the frontier, he slipped round by another route, and stormed Beaune. Beaune was prepared for the attack, and was well fortified; but Mandrin fought his way through, performed his usual deed of releasing smugglers and deserters from the prison, and called on the Mayor. If historians have correctly preserved the little speech he made to the Mayor of Beaune, it was a somewhat theatrical oration, though none the less effective for that:

"I am the famous Mandrin, terror of the farmers-general, and liberator of the people. I have not come as an enemy to the state, to bring you the horrors of war. Beaune is mine, and I could raze it to the ground, but I respect the blood of innocent people. Besides, that is not my purpose. You have two offices here which owe me something. I tax them twenty thousand livres. Make haste and get this money from the officers in charge of the salt and tobacco warehouses. If you hesitate, you will be punished. Tremble for these walls! Fear for yourself!"

The Mayor may have trembled, and feared, but he certainly did not hesitate. In fact, he exceeded the obligations of the vanquished by providing the Mandrins not only with the required money, but with a banquet in their honor. When, after excellent eating, drinking and entertainment, Mandrin went away from Beaune, he left his usual receipt behind him:

"I, the undersigned, Louis Mandrin, acknowledge receipt from Messrs. Saint-Felix and Estienne, bonded warehousemen of the farmers-general in the town of Beaune, of the sum of 20,000 livres, for which the farmers-general have received the bales of tobacco which I have left at the warehouses. At Beaune, the 18th December, 1754.—Louis Mandrin."

Either Mandrin was a genius at timing, or the foe was a fool at it. Eight hours after he left Beaune, Fischer and his cavalry turned up. All they got was the story. Continuing the pursuit, Fischer reached Autun two hours after Mandrin, with another triumph in his pocket, had left it.

Well—better luck next time! Fischer galloped on. Mandrin, anticipating the pursuit, waited for him on the road, having had time to select the best spot for the encounter.

The clash came, and it was a furious one. Was Mandrin to be beaten, at last—just at the end of his successful year? By no means! It is true that he lost several men, and also his hat, but Fischer lost more men—and the battle. The Mandrins, no longer followed, marched triumphantly to Strasbourg.

Here he merely had to announce his name to obtain admittance.

So ended the astonishing year of 1754, and as Mandrin celebrated his victories in Savoy, he continued his ambitious plans for the salvation of France.

One day, at the castle of Rochefort, five deserters from the French army arrived. They begged to be allowed to join the Mandrins, and, following the usual custom with deserters, Mandrin accepted their offer and gave them each ten louis. That night the silence of the castle was suddenly and rudely disturbed. La Morlière's men had got in—admitted by the five alleged deserters—and Lieutenant-Colonel Fischer's cavalry were outside. The authorities had learned, at last, that to beat Louis Mandrin, he had to be surprised and invaded on his own territory.

Mandrin put up a tremendous fight, but the odds were now against him. Once he got away, but he was recaptured, taken to France, tried at Valence, and condemned to be broken at the wheel.

He listened to the verdict without flinching. Throughout the trial he had doggedly refused to give any of his friends away, or to express regret at his behavior. When, in an attempt to rein his boundless spirit, he was told to remember the next world, he became thoughtful for a moment, then asked,

"Tell me, how many inns are there from here to Heaven? I have only six livres to spend *en route*!"

The sentence was carried out on May 26, 1755, in the market place, where he ended his thirty years of eventful life. He was calm to the end, his last words to the executioners being a grim "Get it over quick!"

Smuggling went on in France—and so did the memory of Louis Mandrin.

From a geography textbook, published this century:

"Andorra is a tiny state in the heart of the Pyrenees. Its principal industries are tobacco-growing and smuggling."

Don Smugglo

THE BRITISH mind instinctively associates
smuggling with the coast, since the coast is Britain's only frontier, and, until the advent of the airplane,
contraband—or anything else, for that matter—could
arrive from a foreign land only across the surface of
the sea. But other countries, not entirely surrounded
by water, have other boundaries involving other per-
plexities; and instead of a coast, or in addition to it,
rivers, plains, or mountains have to be guarded against
the contrabandist. When the frontier is mountainous
the customs policemen have a particularly arduous job,
and this is on account not only of the nature of the
locality but the nature of those who inhabit it. Every
environment breeds its special characteristics. Mountains breed boldness, brawn and brigandry.

The mountain smugglers' ship, if it is not his own legs, is his mule or his pony or his horse. He is in his natural element among the crags and crevices, the precipitous passes, and the tortuous tracks. He knows every cave and cavern, he knows every torrent. He has an instinct for the weather and the seasons. He can make the mountains produce comfort for himself and confusion for his enemies, and, unless there is something very unusual or wrong with him, in an emergency he can always reckon on every other mountaineer as a friend.

In no district is all this more true than in the Pyrenees, those mysterious mountains separating Spain from France. This great range has its own smuggling history and personalities, and its own legends. The legends are intriguing though troublesome, for they confuse our perception of the truth, and cloud many a fact with the film of fiction. In describing two of the most famous Pyrenees smugglers—Don Q and Don Sebastian—no attempt will be made here to separate what is undoubtedly true from what is probably true and what is possibly true. The easiest and happiest plan is to believe the lot!

Don Q was a most elusive customer. He knew the Pyrenees as thoroughly as a taximan knows London, and he was just as quick to get about. At one moment he was here, the next there. In the morning he would be reported two days' climb to the west; in the afternoon he would be seen two dayys' climb to the east. He was always popping up where he was least expected, and vanishing from where he was most expected.

If we are to believe all that is told of Don Q—and we have just agreed to do so—he possessed all the virtues attributed to popular rascals. Like Dick Turpin, he was gallant to ladies. Like Robin Hood, he was kind to the poor, and often robbed the rich in order to give to the needy. Like Long John Silver, he had a sense of humor. Like Hereward, he thought it his right to rob the priests. He had been one himself, so he knew they deserved it! One of the best stories about Don Q arises out of his feud with the Church.

The priests were as anxious to catch him as were the *guardias*, and one day, when a friar came upon a party of men who were searching for the smuggler-brigand, he informed them that he could show them where Don Q was. "He will be at my monastery tonight," said the friar. "I know the ruffian's plans, and we should be glad to have your company when we receive him."

The *guardias* were delighted. They themselves had no clue, and they were tired after a long, fruitless search through mountain passes, gloomy ravines, and nerve-racking caverns. A respite in a monastery, where priests always did themselves well, was just what they wanted to revive their tottering faith in the beauty and goodness of life.

The monastery was in a lonely district—in what might be termed perfect Don Q country. The *guardias* visualized their quarry passing along the road with his pack train; they guessed that considerable contraband had passed along this zigzag route. But in the monastery they forgot their arduous job for a while in the pleasures of food and drink and a fire's comfort. They told stories, and their hosts, the priests, told stories just as excellent. Laughter echoed round the solemn walls as they waited for the next visitors, who, the *guardias* swore, would do no laughing.

But the best story was being told by the course of current events. Suddenly the *guardias* stopped laughing. They found themselves looking into the wrong ends of pistols. The priests were holding the pistols. Don Q and his men did not arrive at the monastery— they were already there!

"I promised to show you Don Q," said the jolly priest they had met in the road. "You now behold him."

The *guardias* were outnumbered as well as outmaneuvered. They had to submit, swearing, to being bound.

The alleged priests rode off with triumphant hilarity. Their next halt was at the spot where they had conveyed and bound the real priests. Returning them their borrowed garb, they set the trembling friars back on their road, and told them they would find visitors when they got back. The one good thing Don Q and his fellow scamps missed was the sight of the meeting between the priests and the *guardias*. Still, they doubtless imagined it vividly!

This trick was characteristic of many others. Time after time Don Q set a false trail for the *carabineros* who had got wind of a run of goods, and while they were hopelessly lost in some mountain maze, he was coolly crossing the frontier with his pack mules.

His former monastic experiences proved most helpful. He could always look like the priest he had once been, and as a simple friar pottering round villages or making innocent inquiries in the towns he learned many secrets that gave him the clue to the enemy's plans. "God grant you will catch the fellow," he would murmur. While crossing himself he was devising means of frustrating the pious wish.

Maybe his informant would renew the casual acquaintance a few days later, and, while tied up in a cave, would be cynically chided, "You really should be more careful, my brother. People who talk too much always get into trouble sooner or later. Never talk to a priest in a market place. Avoid the breed like sin!"

Don Sebastian, the other famous Pyrenees smuggler, had a far more sinister atmosphere, though even he, we are assured, was good to the poor and kind to little children. These are the established saving graces of many forms of rascality. His very appearance was akin to the stuff nightmares are made of, and it is doubtful whether he could ever have been passed for a priest. According to the description given by A. Hyatt Verrill in *Smugglers and Smuggling*, almost unbelievable in its completeness, "His lean, bony face with its parchmentlike skin, his bold, keen eyes set deep under bushy brows, his thin cruel lips and his immense hooked nose were startlingly like a bird of prey . . . . His yellow, clawlike fingers with their pointed dirty nails gave his hands the semblance of talons." Add to this a bald head, generally covered

by a wide-rimmed black hat, black clothes concealing
a fragile, attenuated figure, and a sweeping black
mantle, and you have the police description of Don
Sebastian! Every witch seems to have borrowed an
idea from him.

Yet, do not forget, he loved the poor, and babies
were secure in his arms.

It was obvious that such a personality as Don Sebastian should exercise a superstitious as well as a material fear over those he moved among. There is no
record of his origin. This bred the belief that the
origin was supernatural. To ask him, "Where did
you come from?" or "Where were you born?" was
to invite instant removal to that unnamed place! So
nobody asked such questions. He existed. It was left
at that.

But we who have no need to fear his anger at our
curiosity may assume his material origin and make
certain deductions. He probably came of a good family. Evidence pointing to this is found in such facts
as that he was a fluent linguist, speaking half a dozen
languages; that he was an ardent Carlist; and that, in
spite of his physical unattractiveness and disabilities
(although he had great strength he was next door to
being a dwarf), he possessed that indefinable "something" which marked him as a leader.

These facts, too, give some clue to his ultimate appearance in the Pyrenees. The mountainfolk and
Basques were favorable to Don Carlos de Bourbon's
cause and, if politics necessitated the removal of Don

Sebastian from his original home, he might logically seek a new one among people in sympathy with him, as also out of sympathy with the law. Don Sebastian may have regarded his smuggling activities as directed less against Spain than against the Liberals whom he hated. These theories fit in with his policy of secrecy.

There is little doubt, however, that Don Sebastian used the superstition always found in mountain districts to increase his power, and he very soon gained power over many hundreds of men. He did not possess the charm of the American smuggler, Jean Lafitte —far from it!—but like Lafitte he organized the scattered and quarreling smugglers he had dealings with, and formed them into a solid, coherent functioning band, with himself as their leader. He was not known to them as Don Sebastian, but as Quebra Huesos. This implied a breaker of bones and had reference to his vulturelike appearance.

His addresses were countless, though officials who called on him rarely, if ever, found him at home. Had he ordered printed note paper, the headings would have been "A Cave," "A Cottage with Half a Roof," "A Mountain Forest," "A Castle No Longer Occupied (saving by the undersigned)," "The Boulders, Nr. Waterfall"—all, of course, "Somewhere in the Pyrenees." From such addresses, with a few more stable ones, Quebra Huesos organized his huge smuggling industry, and he was never caught.

The *guardias* and *carabineros*, in fact, gave up at last, and the government offered him and his men a free pardon, with all his ill-gotten gains, if he would retire from the business and call it a day. Needless to say, he haughtily refused the kind offer.

His method, when through any mishap his contraband was seized, was simple and effective. In exchange for the contraband he kidnaped an official and claimed a ransom of thrice the value of the goods he had lost. It was not an eye for an eye; it was an ear and a tooth, as well! And he always got what he asked for—saving on one occasion.

We quote the story because no biography of this kind would really be complete without its uplift. It concerns a lady, and reflects Quebra Huesos' excellent attitude toward the fair sex. (It is said that no woman ever came to any harm at either his hands or the hands of his men.) One day the smugglers made a valuable capture. This was the *commandante* of the *guardias* in a border town, a man who for some while had been one of his worst enemies. "Fifty thousand pesos for the return of this prize," went forth the dictum. Safe in his lair, Quebra Huesos and his men waited confidently for the money to turn up. The hostage waited with less hope.

Instead of the money came a girl. She had taken risks to come, and all the smugglers agreed that she was as beautiful as she was brave. She did not bring a centavo with her. She brought a story instead. It was of the hostage's wife—her mother—who had fallen ill through despair and agony. She had tried in vain to raise the ransom money, but had found the amount too large.

Don Sebastian was touched. Let us hope he would have been equally touched if the girl had had a squint, a hump, and a limp. Father and daughter were given a safe-conduct home at a sole cost of wear and tear to their shoe leather.

There is another story of this mountain smuggler which proves he did not reserve all his help for the beautiful. He came upon an old mountaineer who had slipped on a rough track, fallen, and broken his leg. Two of his men carried the casualty back to his hut, but more than that was needed. The next immediate necessity was a surgeon, and a good one.

The old man could not send for the medical aid he required. The surgeon might have jibbed at the journey, even if he had been summoned, for he would have found small pecuniary recompense at the end of it. Such, anyhow, was Don Sebastian's low opinion of the breed. To make sure of the matter, and to avoid the delay or argument of bargaining, he went to the nearest town and kidnaped the best surgeon he could find. The scared and indignant man was hauled to the patient's hut, and he set the broken limb while his kidnaper sat and watched him with pistols on knees. Then, lest the surgeon should think ill of him, Don Sebastian gave him a bag of gold which represented ten times the normal fee and sent the astonished man home again. The bone-setter did not ask the bone-breaker how he had got the gold. He accepted it, to soothe his nerves, as an astonishing gift from Heaven.

But he deserved his recompense. It must have

been a very trying operation, since the surgeon knew that if he had failed he might never have got home at all. When bad luck came to any of Quebra Huesos' men, or to anyone under his protection, worse luck followed for the person who had brought it. A bullet, or a knife, or a gentle push over a precipice—it was quite simple.

Don Sebastian departed from the Pyrenees as mysteriously as he came! Again, in this point he resembled Jean Lafitte. Or perhaps this is one of the recognized historical patterns for strange characters whose memories are confused with legend. We hate to see the invincible brought low! Sentiment attempts to conceal the facts before they can harden. Was Hereward ever really conquered, to become the vassal of William of Normandy? Perish the thought! And perish the possibility that Don Sebastian, smuggler-prince of the Pyrenees, could have met some sticky end, bound and taunted as he had bound and taunted others!

He vanished. That is enough. If we want to reinforce this romantic inconclusion with logic, we may remember that he was a Carlist, and that there were many plots and risings that could have tempted him away, in the hope that a new government would arise to protect, and not to plunder. It is better to think that Don Sebastian died fighting in the cause of Don María Izador Carlos de Bourbon than that he perished in defense of contraband.

But in the mysterious fastnesses of the Pyrenees you will still find folk who deride either theory, and who believe that the vulturelike dwarf with the clawlike fingers, and the hooked nose and beetle-brows and bald head, was gathered back into the occult regions from which he was evolved.

Lately there has been another form of smuggling across the Pyrenees—arms one way and refugees the other. But perhaps this is too grimly recent to bear enlargement in the present volume.

Mr. Punch's definition of coast-guard stations:

"Castles of idleness, where able-bodied men spend their time in looking through long glasses for imaginary smugglers."

Enter the Coast Guard

THE DEFEAT of Napoleon in 1815 had
many consequences, and one of the consequences
was the coast guard. When Napoleon went out, coast
guards came in, occupying the Martello towers that
had been built to repel the anticipated French invasion.

The coast guard was not a new idea. He was
evolved from an old idea that had never worked, and
for a while he did not work either, save in the sense
of sometimes doing eighteen hours' duty per day. He
was not even called a coast guard when he put his
first telescope to his eye and looked for his first smug-

gler, being born into the troubled world somewhat muddily out of confusion of changes. Let us trace him from his origin.

At the end of the seventeenth century, the coast was guarded, very inadequately, by riding officers. One riding officer to four miles of coast did not go a very long way toward putting a ring round Great Britain. This being pointed out at the commencement of the eighteenth century—in 1703, to be exact—permission was granted to the riding officers to call upon the dragoons when circumstances warranted. This was never a popular or satisfactory arrangement. The dragoons hated serving under the riding officers, who were not strictly military, hated their additional work when it came along, hated the meager addition of twopence a day to their wages, and seem in fact to have hated everything about the whole business barring the bribes which they not infrequently accepted from the smugglers.

The riding officers were as unpopular with the military gods as with the military minions, and many obstacles and delays were put in their way when they called for the required assistance. Yet this ridiculous state of things continued, with various minor modifications, for over a century—till 1822. "Between the devil and the deep sea" was a term well understood by these despairing men.

They formed the land army of excisemen whose job it was to deal with the land-smugglers. The sea army, or the exciseman's navy, comprised the revenue cutters whose job it was to deal with the sea-smug-

RIDING OFFICER AND DRAGOONS

glers. In its way, their job was just as hard and just
as unsuccessful. At first it was a question of whales
chasing eels. Then, as the revenue cutters improved,
so did the smuggling luggers and galleys, and in each
improvement the smuggler was always ahead of the
revenue man. Naturally both the revenue men at sea
and the excisemen on shore had their successes. The
smugglers could have done very well without them.
But the smugglers also did very well with them, and
won far more encounters than they lost.

In fifteen average encounters they needed only five
successes to pay their way. They obtained twelve—
four times the required number!

When, however, the seemingly endless wars that
had given smuggling its golden opportunity came actually to their conclusion—when Spain and the Neth-
erlands no longer had to be thought about, when
America had gained her independence (through a
little matter of tea), when Waterloo wrote "finis" to
over a century of conflict with France and Napoleon
stepped onto St. Helena one mid-October day, never
to leave it—the British government took a long
breath, looked at its useless Martello towers, and suddenly realized how these beach-forts could be utilized.

And then England really took off its coat to smite
the smuggler.

Its first blow was the Blockade. In the words of
the boxing commentator, there was not much force
behind it and it did no damage, but it prepared the
way for other blows. The Blockade was supervised
by two warships whose duty it was to cover the coasts

of Kent and Sussex. The *Ramillies,* seventy-four guns, was stationed in the Downs; the *Hyperion,* forty-two guns, was stationed at Newhaven. The former was a famous ship and had twice been narrowly missed by torpedoes in the American war. Then it had been commanded by Sir Thomas Hardy, but now its boss was a severe Scotsman who earned the title of "Old Jock McCulloch," and who dealt very sternly with defaulters. Members of the crews were landed at the Martello towers, and at other small Blockade stations specially built when the towers were not sufficient.

The rest of the coast was still left to the revenue cutters, but their system was altered to fall, as far as possible, into line. Men were detached to form boats' crews, who had to watch the most vulnerable parts of the coast at night. Lacking the quarters supplied by the Martello towers and the Blockade stations, they had the rougher time. When the weather was too bad for patrolling the sea—this was called "guard-row-ing"—they had to haul their boat into some creek or haven and convert their sail into a rough tent.

It was soon quite obvious that these new arrangements were not going to stop smuggling. The men in the Martello towers and Blockade stations of Kent and Sussex were under naval discipline, but Old Jock McCulloch was kept busy dealing with cases of inefficiency, negligence, desertion or worse, while the boats' crews from the revenue cutters had such a miserable time of it, and were held in such contempt, that they frequently drowned their sorrows in the liquor they were engaged to suppress.

Doubtless the boats' crews grumbled. Old Jock was too far east to cast his restraining shadow over them, and the officers under whom they served—naval officers, civilian officers and deputation officers, a mixed lot—were not as expert as the fiery Scotsman in the art of dressing down. Why were they treated like this? They wanted to know. Why didn't they have proper quarters like the other chaps? How could you remain efficient if, when winter storms drove your boat ashore, the only protection you had against the weather was your own dripping sails? Was it reasonable?

It was thoroughly unreasonable, and their prayers were answered. Old hulks were commandeered, and houses were hired, to provide them with shore headquarters, while to reduce their inferiority complexes they were now called the "Preventive Water Guard." Even under that impressive title, however, they often found it hard to induce anyone to let them a house, and a passage in Couch's *History of Polperro* runs:

> Though active opposition was not politic, the people determined, one and all, to offer as much passive resistance as was safe. No one would let a coastguardman a house to live in at any price; so the whole force was obliged to make a dwelling and guardhouse of the hull of a vessel, which was moored to the old quay.

Couch refers to the men as coastguardmen, but at that time the term was a loose designation, and did not become the permanent official title till a few years later.

The organization was progressing, but it still had some distance to go. There was a breach here and an overlapping there, and dismissals for one offense or another remained disturbingly frequent. The smugglers took advantage of every flaw.

One of the flaws was the quality of the material from which the various official bodies drew many of their recruits. The tinker, the tailor, and the candlestick-maker could all get jobs without either technical or ethical qualifications. Another flaw was confusion of control. The Army, the Navy and the Board of Customs each had a finger in the pie. So in 1822 a Consolidation Order gave full control to the Board of Customs, saving in the case of the Blockade men. If a customs officer had bossed a battleship, the battleship would have sunk in shame! But the dragoons were dispensed with—released from a hundred and nineteen years of unwilling service—and the riding officers, rechristened the Mounted Guard, became a definite department of the Blockade stations, representing their movable force.

Another reform was that the Mounted Guards, late riding officers, and now alternatively known as "Horse Policemen," no longer accepted recruits from civilian sources, while a certain interest was shown in the retiring age of officers. Men with long records of earnest service were not immediately dispensed with, but the *Sussex Advertiser* reported a few years later that three

members of the Mounted Guard belonging to the
Arundel district had just been superannuated on full
salaries. Their ages were seventy-two, eighty, and
eighty-four! . . .

And so, at last, to the important years of 1829 to
1831, when a central-control Coastguard Office was
established in London, a triple cordon of defense made
three live rings, one inside the other, between the
smuggler and his goal, the old Blockade was discon-
tinued, and the British coast guard as we know him in
picture, prose, and patriotic poetry came into being.

His was a real triumph, slowly and painfully
achieved. He had swallowed, and more or less di-
gested, the riding officers and the dragoons behind
him, the revenue cutters and boats' crew and Preventive Water Guard ahead of him; he had even swallowed the Blockade and Old Jock McCulloch. In due
course he was himself swallowed by the Royal Navy,
but that is another story which did not begin until—
in his own opinion—he had put smugglers down for
the count.

Others may hold other views regarding the credit
for the smuggler's final eclipse. Free trade, in an un-
piratical sense, may have had something to do with
it! In 1842 Sir Robert Peel introduced an income tax
of 7*d.* for three years (!), and to alleviate this unusual
burden, began lowering or removing tariffs. The
smuggler himself attributed his decline to the informer. Riding officers? Revenue cutters? Dragoons? Blockades? Even coast guards? Psh! Given
a square deal against the law, he'd have downed the

lot! But what can an honest smuggler do when the country is poisoned with spies? When informers are as numerous as slugs after rain?

To all of which the British coast guard listened with tolerant national humor, and then, when the noise was over, raised his telescope to see what he could see. And we may forgive him if the magnified circle of his vision was mainly filled with his own importance, because in that sense we are nearly all of us coast guards, seeing very little more than ourselves.

Lest it should be imagined that the coast guard did nothing but stand outside a neat, whitewashed house in a trim cliff-garden and look at himself through a telescope bought for him by a taxpayer, let us pass into his skin and imagine ourselves a coast guard of a hundred years ago. We shall be very content to pass out of the skin again.

We shall, of course, have to reverse the customary order of things by generally sleeping in the day and working in the night. The coast guard was mainly a night watchman, and when he was observed staring through his telescope in the sunlight he was merely enjoying one of his periodic respites. Perhaps once every ten days he was allowed this relief. As he enjoyed such occasions—although even then he had to keep his telescope eye well open—so he enjoyed, each lunar month, the five nights of which the middle brought the full moon. The moon was better for snuggling than smuggling, and during these periods night patrolling was relaxed a little, and was also pleasanter. You could see things coming. There was less chance of being leaped on from the back and finding your windpipe squeezed before you could draw your cutlass or summon assistance with your blue light.

On the average night, when you roused yourself from your day's slumber, had your meal and allowance of grog, and sallied forth at dusk with your cutlass, your brace of pistols inside your greatcoat, your blue light, and your rump-stool—a one-legged chair to which, when you wanted to sit down and think, you added your own two legs to form a tripod—you were never certain that you would come back again. The odds, certainly, were in your favor, but you remembered poor old Charlie who was toppled over a cliff only a fortnight ago, and poor old Tom who had looked so nasty that time you came upon him on the shingle.

Of course, if trouble did arise, and God looked after you, your night's work might entitle you to a pretty reward. For goods seized you would get a percentage of such portion as was allocated to your station, your amount depending upon your rating. The chief officer got twenty-five shares; the lowest rating was six shares. Or you might take a smuggler single-handed and earn £20 blood money. £20! The chance of that was worth a few unpleasant thrills up your spine!

On the other hand, if God was not looking after you, you would probably be (*a*) very severely reprimanded; (*b*) dismissed; or (*c*) killed, like poor old Charlie and Tom. Nice chap, Tom. Used to make you laugh. Charlie didn't matter so much.

What was this night's work going to be? You never knew beforehand. Smugglers were so slippy at discovering the routine that it had to be varied constantly, and even the coast guards themselves did not know their orders till they were assembled in the watch house and their officer told them off to their particular duties and guards—the "guard" being the stretch of coast for which they were responsible. Or it might be boat work, "creeping" or "sweeping" for a crop of goods believed to have been sunk in the neighborhood till the smugglers could call for it. In that case you had to try to give them a disappointment by collecting it first.

But there is no fishing for sunk tubs of liquor tonight on an inky sea. You know that much before your officer instructs you, and you know one thing more! You will not have the same guard as you had last night. Never the same twice running. You might have met a smuggler last night and promised to turn the other way! . . .

Oh—so *that's* where you are to go? You might have guessed it! You spotted the new moon through a looking glass, and that always meant bad luck. . . . The bit of beach where you'd come across Tom.

You mustn't tell anybody. No chance of a bit of sympathy. One of your orders is that, after having received your instructions, you must not speak to a soul. The men on either side of you will come in response to your blue light if you summon them, and if they are not too far away, but you won't know who they are till they turn up.

Well, off to your beach. You haven't got to worry about the inland lanes. The Mounted Guard will look after them and report anything suspicious, but your own bit of England is quite long enough. Nearly a mile of it. A mile of pebbles. Pebbles make the hell of a noise. You can't walk for sixteen hours on your toes.

This is going to be one of the long sessions. Midwinter, when there's no clear light from four in the afternoon till eight next morning. Not till dawn will you be relieved by the day watchman.

There is no need to provide a horrible incident for the particular night you have chosen to enter the coast guard's skin. You have merely done this to experience his ordinary routine, not to taste his really bad times. The routine is bad enough as the pebbles crunch under your boots or as you sit on your rump-stool to shelter

from a wintry blast in a cliff angle, watching the dark sea wake into little lines of white, across which flit the shadows of your imagination. You meet nobody, but you have one constant companion. Tom's ghost.

At dawn, the day watchman relieves you.

"Anything?" he asks.

"Nothing," you report.

Tom's ghost is your private concern.

If you are a lucky man, you may have a wife to return to, but even women are rationed by the strict coast-guard regulations. In the 1830's, a coast guard with elaborate ideas was dismissed from the services for the offense of "having two wives, and families by each."

It was due to a proposal of Mrs. Fry in 1833 that coast guards were provided with "libraries of books of an entertaining and moral tendency." Truthfully or untruthfully, a minor poet has informed us of the sequel.

Quoth that excellent dame, Mrs. Fry:
"The life of our coast guards is dry!"
    So she sent them good books
    Of the downfall of crooks
And the ghastly results of a lie.

The coast guards whose minds required feeding
With novels of taste and of breeding
    Turned over the pages
    By slow painful stages,
Then from Cornwall to Kent gave up reading.

The Feminine Touch

A CUSTOMS officer recently expressed this
view:

"Women are natural smugglers. In fact, smuggling is more natural to them than it is to men. No
woman can resist a bargain, and most of them seem
to consider it as a sort of moral right. I have known
women who could afford to keep three motorcars lie
like troopers to save half a dollar of duty! Wrong?
They don't seem to think it is. They see no more
harm in smuggling than their husbands see in diddling
the income tax!"

We may take this official view with a grain of salt.
There are husbands who pay their income tax like
good little boys, even if they wince while they do so.
The officer whose remarks have been quoted had just
been instrumental in getting a lady heavily fined, so

he was rather close to his subject. Still, if statistics could produce the figure, the number of women who, while they would never cheat at cards or steal your purse, delight in hoodwinking a customs officer, would probably play havoc with our ethical faith.

According to our disillusioned official, "The Atlantic's full of them!" So, in this sense, is the English Channel.

The case which produced the official's little outburst certainly provided an excuse for it. A charming American made the Atlantic crossing two or three times a year. She had a wealthy husband, who gave her more money than she knew what to do with, and she had no financial need to exploit her ingenuity or her charm. But she was a "natural smuggler." She profited by man's gallantry and weakness, and the customs officer admitted that, for several years, he and others were duped by her ingenuous, disarming smile.

But one day, the "unknown quantity" tripped her up. A friend of the customs officer heard her creating a bon mot out of her triumphs. "My 'hide' is my skin," she said. So, on the next occasion, the disarming smile had no effect. The good lady was handed over to a stern female and forced to strip, and she had to pay duty on some of her excellent superfluous figure.

She was by no means the first woman, though she was one of the cleverest, to improve on the shape God gave her. One woman improved on it so extensively that her unsuspecting husband, imagining it was her taste for European dishes that had increased her avoirdupois, decided to play a little joke on her as their ship reached New York. He took a customs officer aside and pointed out his wife. "You see that lady?" he whispered. "From what I have heard, I guess she will be worth your study."

He deserved what he got. The study produced countless yards of lace wound round her portly body, and as her purchases had impoverished her, the husband had to pay the piper! Probably this was the last practical joke he ever played on anybody.

Silk—lace—lingerie—model frocks—all these are smuggled into England today across the Channel, and many a woman owes the lightness of her clothing bill to the illicit ingenuity of another member of her sex, and to her studious avoidance of asking leading questions. This Channel smuggling is not always successful, however. A well-known woman recently had to pay thousands of pounds through a slip that gave her away. Another, when questioned regarding a number of dutiable articles concealed in her trunk, declared that she had merely hidden them there to conceal them from her husband, who was traveling with her. She wished to surprise him with the gifts on his birthday! The gifts proved, by the time the final account was settled, exceedingly expensive ones.

It is, of course, only in comparatively modern times —since smuggling became a gentle art—that woman has indulged her smuggling fancy to this extent. In the more robust era when smugglers risked not merely fines, but death, women confined themselves mainly to benefiting by the system, not participating in it. Still, even then, there were a few hardy women who risked life and limb by engaging in the actual business.

One of the most famous of these women smugglers concealed her true identity under the name of Montmorillon. As with the Lafitte brothers, her origin is wrapped in mystery; and mystery being the mother of invention, all sorts of stories have been invented about this astonishing smuggleress. As, for instance:

(1) She was a member of a noble French family. The noble French family was robbed by a less noble French government of its estates, which should have passed to her. Her husband was murdered. Love, lucre, and livelihood having all been wrested from her, she changed her identity, and decided to cheat as she had been cheated, and to pay her way by getting her own back. This is a plausible story, but perhaps its weakness is that no list would be complete without something of the sort!

(2) She was English. She hated the English government—whether with just cause or not is left open. She became a smuggler to defraud the English customs and express her loathing.

(3) She was a naturally adventurous woman, who loved the sea and lived for adventure, and who would have screamed with boredom if she had been set to do common, ordinary tasks on land.

(4) Her father was a smuggler, so she became one.

(5) She was found in a barrel by a fisherman of Brittany. The barrel floated in on the tide, and the baby it preserved was the only item saved from the wreck of a smugglers' ship. The fisherman brought

the baby up till one day the baby—now in her teens—
vanished, called mysteriously to the trade of her dead
parent. The baby reappeared as Montmorillon.

Number 5 is the most attractive and original, but
numbers 3 and 4 seem more likely, and probably the
truth was a combination of these two.

Whatever her origin, Montmorillon's hideaway
was near St. Malo, and she became a very remarkable
personage. There was nothing small about her or her
enterprises. Her interest was big game, and whenever
her large brig was sighted and recognized by "the
enemy," nerves became tenser and wits quickened.
There was sure to be some fun, but the one who
laughed last was almost certain to be Montmorillon.
She showed the enemy her heels, or, if she could not
run fast enough, her teeth. Montmorillon was a
fighter, and here is one story to prove that she did not
fight only to save her own skin.

In an engagement with a cruiser, Montmorillon's
crew got the worst of it—for a change—and some of
the men were captured. The prisoners were conveyed
to the English coast, and spent their first night of
captivity on board, in the harbor where the cruiser
was lying.

The silence of the night was broken by soft sounds.
The still water of the harbor became full of little
ripples. A shadowy shape loomed below the shadowy
shape of the cruiser itself. Then numerous smaller
shadowy shapes swarmed up the ship and boarded her.
One was Montmorillon.

To the glory of her name, if not to the glory of

the British Navy, Montmorillon effected a swift capture of the ship. The overpowered crew were bound and put into boats, and the boats were shoved out into the harbor. In the morning the boats and their unhappy occupants were found but the cruiser had vanished. It was well on its way to St. Malo.

Cornishmen chuckled when they heard the story. Montmorillon was one of their most popular figures. Time after time they took their luggers to the Channel Isles, found Montmorillon waiting for them with a good cargo of contraband from St. Malo, paid her price, and returned with their spoils to their Cornish coves, to brighten the palates and lighten the pockets of Cornish tipplers.

Montmorillon did not hoard her gold. She gave much of it to the poor. This does not dispose of the theory that she was a member of a noble French family who had lost her estates, yet if she had been she might have used her new wealth to buy the estates back again. There would have been some irony in the process.

A woman smuggler of equal fame was Bessie Catchpole.

There is no mystery about her origin. She lived in the early nineteenth century, and she was a smuggler's wife. Her husband owned the yawl *Sally*, and plied his trade successfully till one day he lost an encounter with preventive men. In a desperate tussle he was killed.

This would have cured the average woman of any taste for smuggling, but Bessie was far from an average woman. Instead of spending her days in mourning and remorse, she dedicated them to her husband's memory and carried on his trade. She did this so completely that she even emulated his mode of dress and his habits.

An incident on the very first day established her firmly in his shoes. Dressed in man's attire, with a cutlass at her side and a pipe between her lips, she appeared before her late husband's astonished crew. They stared at the unusual sight, and one of the men broke into loud laughter. Bessie was a wise woman as well as a brave one. She recognized that her whole future might depend on how she handled the moment. She walked up to the hilarious sailor, pointed out that he was laughing at his skipper, and then gave him a straight left to the jaw. He was knocked out—perhaps by astonishment as well as by the strength of the blow—and Bessie bossed her men from that day onward.

In spite of her physical courage, she seems to have been less ready for a definite scrap with revenue cutters than was Montmorillon, and to have preferred strategy when she could achieve it. One evening a revenue boat appeared on the horizon, like a policeman round a corner. Bessie had a cargo of brandy, but she did not run. She could not, for there was not sufficient wind; and shortly afterward the wind dropped altogether, and both ships were becalmed.

Darkness came. The black wall of night separated the cutter from the *Sally*. Getting her casks of brandy on board, Bessie had them fastened together with

BESSIE CATCHPOLE AND HER CREW

grapplings and floats and then lowered into the sea.

The black wall melted into the gray of morning, and as the sun rose, a boat slipped from the cutter's side and brought unwelcome visitors. But Bessie acted as though they were quite welcome. It was an honor to have revenue officers turn up for breakfast, and she invited them to the meal! They refused curtly, having come to look for something very different from bacon and eggs. They looked, of course, in vain, and returned empty-handed. Bessie, on the contrary, did not return empty-handed. She chased the floating barrels, regained them, and returned with all her good French brandy.

This was, of course, an old trick, and to have got away with it Bessie must have been fortunate, or the revenue officers must have been incompetent. A later ruse was more original. When its victim, the revenue boat, came in sight, she hoisted a yellow handkerchief and sailed direct for it. The revenue officers gave the *Sally* the widest berth possible. They preferred failure to the plague!

Hardly cricket, this. Still, there is not much cricket in smuggling, and Bessie had to complete her journey from Dunkirk to Ipswich.

For a couple of years she played hide-and-seek with the harassed revenue men, and one of her favorite ruses was the "two-sail trick." She carried two complete sets of sails, white and buff. When she knew she was "wanted," and had last been identified by the white sails, she changed to the buff and fooled the watchers' telescopes. When the telescopes were scanning the horizon for buff sails, she changed back to white. Other smugglers played this trick, but none more effectively or neatly than Bessie Catchpole.

By one of those odd coincidences for which there seems neither rhyme nor reason, Catchpole was the name of another woman connected with smuggling history. Margaret, immortalized in the story of the Rev. Richard Cobbold, was related to Bessie only by her associations.

Margaret was not herself a smuggler. She had the misfortune to love a man who was—Will Laud, a member of Captain Bargood's Gang. Bargood was a particularly bad character, with headquarters at Bawdsey Cliffs, near Felixstowe, and during fifteen years of successful smuggling on the east coast he was never caught. The same could not be said, however, of those who worked for him, and Will Laud got into plenty of hot water. Margaret did more for him than he deserved, nursing his wounds and trying to reform him. His response was to shower her with presents obtained by the very means she criticized.

Then Margaret herself committed an offense. Will, having temporarily given up his bad ways, returned to them, and begged her to come and see him. To do this she used somebody else's horse, and as horse-stealing was a capital crime she was sentenced to death. The penalty was reduced to a term of seven years' imprisonment, and in prison she again met Will Laud, serving a lesser term for debt. When he was free he rescued Margaret from jail, but they were overtaken near Ipswich, and Will was shot through the heart.

For the second time Margaret was sentenced to death, and for the second time she was reprieved. The alternative now, however, was transportation for life. She ended her days in Australia, twelve thousand miles from the scenes of her tragic life.

One more woman must be mentioned, the mother of the famous Will Watch whose exploits have been told in verse, in a play, and in a three-volume novel. Mrs. Watch once aided and abetted her son in a very definite manner. After being imprisoned for the murder of an excise officer whom he had carried out to sea and flung overboard, Will was tried at Highcliff, and pronounced guilty by the Recorder, Mr. Keswick. It was an unpopular verdict, as were the majority of verdicts unfavorable to smugglers, and even the jury who had assisted in his downfall joined in signing a petition to George III for his pardon!

But mothers cannot wait for kings. Mrs. Watch did not wait. Gathering a crowd of sympathizers, she stormed the prison, climbed a ladder, and smashed a way in through the roof. Will was rescued, quite undeservedly, and managed to reach his pet cave of chalk, when he defied such members of the British Army as were collected to recapture him by hurling down chalk upon their heads!

The history of smuggling is packed with amazing feats. It is a curious fact, and one into which perhaps we should not inquire too closely, that the amazing feats were nearly all performed by the smugglers, while those who tried to capture them were often only amazing for their infinite capacity for failure!

THE FEMALE SMUGGLER

With her pistols loaded she went on board,
By her side hung a glittering sword,
In her belt two daggers—well arm'd for war,
Was the Female Smuggler, who never fear'd a scar.

(The author of this poem is unknown; but the
verse, which was published over a century ago, is
headed: "A. Ryle, Printer, 2 & 3, Monmouth Court,
7 Dials.")

The American Problem

IF THE original English smugglers had their excuse, the excuse of the original American smugglers was far greater—which is not to say that they
would not have smuggled, in any case! As a matter
of sad fact, when their excuse weakened toward the
end of the eighteenth century, smuggling showed no
sign of following suit, and a practice that had been
largely fanned by local patriotism and a very legitimate
sense of injustice found ample subsequent fuel in human greed and selfishness. Nevertheless, it was the
rebellion against unjust legislation, as mainly expressed
in smuggling, that led at last to July 4, 1776.

One of the earliest examples of this unjust legislation was the First Navigation Act of Charles II. This

Act was passed in 1660, at about the time when the English "owlers" were enjoying their final heyday, and it struck a severe blow to the trade of the American colonists. Charles II had no grudge against his colonials across the Atlantic, but as he invariably thought in terms of self, he could never see much farther than his own nose. The Act ordained that, ,from April 1, 1661, sugar, tobacco, wool, cotton and various other essential commodities were barred from being conveyed from the English plantations in America to any foreign territory.

The result of this was that the American colonists were forced either to become smugglers or to languish through impossible trade conditions. They chose, naturally enough, not to languish. Foreign trade was essential to their welfare, and in the West Indies, among the Dutch, Spanish, and French possessions, they found ample opportunity for running contraband. Legal phraseology evolved three thousand miles away was not going to prevent them.

In these circumstances it is not surprising that smuggling flourished; and the advent of rum gave a tremendous fillip to colonial prosperity. Rum came from molasses. Molasses came from the sugar cane. The sugar cane came from plantations, the plantations were worked by negro slaves, and the negro slaves were bought on the African coast for rum. What an ironically vicious circle! The slaves minted the currency that purchased them!

Some quaint remarks on both negroes and rum, before the latter had come fully into its own, are contained in Thomas Tenison's *Philosophical Letters upon Several Occasions,* written in 1684.

Now the Scums, Dregs and excrementations Parts which are separated from the finer and more essential Parts, in making of Sugar are of some value, for from the same being fermented and distilled, is extracted a strong Spirit which they call Rumm; so that you see Sir that the Juice of the Cane, by Art and extream Labour is made into three considerable commodities, viz., Sugar, Treacle and Rumm, besides which the Servants and Negroes make a very good drink with Molasses Water and some Ginger worked up altogether, the Strength being according to the Quantity of Molasses put in . . . and this drink is called by the Indian name of Coow Woow.

Coow Woow was cheaper than rum, but in spite of this advantage it soon dropped out of the white man's dictionary, whereas rum came to stay.

But Thomas Tenison was not only interested in the rum itself. Being a man ahead of his times, he was more interested in the poor wretches whose unremunerated labor placed the drink within reach of the white man's mouth and purse. Yet it will be noted that, in the following extract from his letters, he realizes the futility of urging humanity for humanity's sake, and makes use of the practical argument. This form of logic, of course, was not peculiar to his own generation.

And now give me leave to tell you Sir [he writes] nothing has been more hurtful and injurious to your Plantations than the unkind

Usage and hard Labour you put your Black
Women to, whose preservation, health and
strength, you ought to have made your main
Study: But you on the contrary, have doubled
their Burdens and what you unwarily design for
their preservation manifestly leads to their Di-
struction; for tho' after those intollerable Works
and Fatigues you give them Rum which at present
is a little refreshing, yet you cannot but know it is
distructive to Nature, wasting the Vitals, and an
Enemy of Propagation; So much of it in respect
to Women Kind. I am loath to be particular with
you Sir, in respect to Negro Men, and your ply-
ing of them with this distructive Liquor; and that
upon Sundays too, to very bad purpose: And tho'
your Intention herein be to perpetuate their
Servitude, etc. the very Methods you take to do it,
by such indulging of them in this excess of drinking, at the same time proves very frequently your
Disappointment, and their Death: And as you
cannot be convinced of the truth thereof, so I appeal to your own experience, whether your allow-
ing of Polygamy, or plurality of Wives to your
Black Slaves, doth in any way answer your end
in the multiplication of Servants thereby, I very
much doubt the contrary, and that 'tis the ready
way to lose both the Root and the Branch, nothing
being more Destructive to Humane Nature than
the Immoderate use of Venery, which upon the
persecuting of a fresh Object, etc. is usually pro-
voked beyond all due bounds, to the manifest
enervation and decay of the Man, from whom no
vigorous Issue can be expected; and if any at all
seldom or never comes to Maturity.

Tenison did not belong to the easy-thinking class
who, in every generation, adopt the simple line that

the correct thing to do is what the other fellow does,
and whose lazy philosophy has been aptly expressed
in these lines:

> Why prate of black and white,
> If people fight, we'll fight;
> If people cease,
> We'll plump for peace—
> Whatever is, is right!

That outlook forms the main obstacle to real
progress. While the minority spiritual attitude is
struggling to become the majority practical rule, it has
to meet all the specious arguments on the way.

Modern smugglers defend themselves by pointing
to their vast numerical company. The old slave-
merchants and rum-runners, when they troubled about
a defense at all, used just the same sort of excuse,
adding that once the negroes were transplanted they
were perfectly content. This apparent contentment
(and it was not invariably apparent) was not due to
any instinctive happiness in their condition, but to the
traditional subjectiveness and philosophy of their race.
You do not help yourself by banging your head against
a brick wall unless there is some reasonable prospect
of displacing a few of the bricks.

Of course all slaveowners were not unkind. Many
of the negroes found humane masters, and it is refreshing to read of two slaves, a man and a woman, who
were enabled to earn money, and who worked and
scraped and saved till they had collected between two
or three hundred pounds. But they did not remain
and spend it in their new land. They bought their

freedom, and returned to the land from which they had been stolen.

By the 1720's, rum was overtaking cider as a popular commodity. By the 1730's, cider was an "also ran." Then came the first Molasses Act, of 1733, with its far-reaching consequences. It struck a blow at rum by limiting its markets, as the First Navigation Act of Charles II had done with other articles. The rum-rich and the rum-dependent were told, in effect, that they must not trade in the cheapest markets without paying ruinously for the privilege of doing so.

If the cheapest markets had been the English plantations, with which the American colonists were now expected to deal almost exclusively, there would have been no complaints. Patriotism was quite ready to express itself even at a distance of three thousand miles. But the cheapest markets, on which the prosperity of the American traders depended, were the foreign plantations; particularly the French ones, for this reason. France had also introduced stringent laws and, in order to protect her own home industries, would not allow rum and molasses to be imported from her own overseas possessions. This naturally created a glut of those articles in the French plantations, and a glut always reduces prices for those able and willing to purchase the surplus. The American colonists were able and willing, which suited everybody but the English government.

"Why should we sacrifice ourselves for the English government?" demanded the American colonists, when the Molasses Act came along to confound them.

"Why should we limit our earnings to line the pockets of English shopkeepers? What are the government and the shopkeepers doing for us?"

There might have been an answer to those questions, but the answer was by no means obvious.

So practically everybody became a smuggler, and a smuggler with precious few conscience pricks. The situation was comparable with that created a century and a half later by Prohibition. Public morality fell with a swoop, though perhaps it had not quite so far to fall. Laws were flouted, order was derided. This is what inevitably happens when a government institutes an unpopular law it cannot enforce. A blow is struck against constitutional authority, and just as one lie in private life leads to another, so the breaking of one law in national life leads to the breaking of another, or the breaking of one treaty in international life leads to international chaos. Jones cheats Smith. Smith scratches his head and cheats Robinson. And Robinson calls upon Jones and walks out with the teaspoons.

In judging this particular situation it should be remembered that the American colonists were originally a very law-abiding people, with ideals well ahead of their times. Although they possessed their share of human failings, they were not traditional smugglers, and would have preferred to expand their trade by lawful methods. Naturally, once the ball began rolling, it gathered all the dirt and mud on the way.

England tried to coat the pill. "This is only a tem-

porary measure, to get us round a little corner," she
assured the colonists in 1735. "Just for five years. Five
years isn't long, is it?" At the end of the five years,
in 1738, she said the same thing all over again. The
little corner had not been rounded. It would take
five years longer. The speech was repeated in 1743,
and again in 1748. It became a serial story. A serial
story which no one believed.

The outbreak of war with France brought fresh
complications. The crime of the rum-runner now
grew graver, for smuggling became an international
matter, and the American colonist communed with
himself again. Studying his face to see whether it retained any aspect of honesty.

"This war is a nuisance," he reflected. "I wouldn't
care to be ruled by the French, certainly, but it isn't
so much fun being ruled by the English, either. I
wonder what would happen if we ruled ourselves?
Someday, maybe, we shall! Meanwhile, I'm sorry,
George III, but I've got to earn my living!"

So the smuggling went on, and the smugglers'
boats still slipped to and from foreign ports.

With a grim touch of irony, the conflict which
might have stopped smuggling provided it with fresh
opportunities. When prisoners of war were exchanged
they formed a most useful link in the chain of illicit
trade, and they were used to smuggle goods from the
land they had been imprisoned in. John and Jacques
might be international enemies, but they were quite
ready to do a little private trade.

Nor were the captains of the ships that returned the

prisoners to their respective shores averse from making a dishonest penny or two. As a matter of fact, they made a considerable number of pennies by arranging with the local port-authorities that their special permits should not be delivered up and canceled after the one privileged voyage for which they had been issued. These permits were auctioned, and sold to the highest bidder—to be used afterward not for prisoners, but for contraband!

Idealists—for they existed—flung up their despairing hands and wept!

In 1763 the situation with France eased. That particular war, or that particular phase of it, was over, and a psychological moment arrived when wise and understanding diplomacy might have worked wonders. But England at that time was not suffering from a surfeit of intelligence. Instead of offering the olive branch to her American colonials, she offered—a second Molasses Act!

Rum, a West-Indian Drink stronger than Brandy, drawn from Dreggs of Sugar for the most part, yet sometimes from Fruits, and Rows of Fish.

From *"A New Dictionary of the Terms, Ancient and Modern, of the Canting Crew"* (*1700*)

Rum I take to be the name which unwashed moralists apply alike to the product distilled from molasses and the noblest juices of the vineyard.

OLIVER WENDELL HOLMES
The Autocrat of the Breakfast Table

Last Voyage of the VISION

THE CAPTAIN pored over his instructions, to be quite sure that he understood them. He had been given the command of the schooner *Vision*, with a crew that seemed to exceed her normal needs, and a couple of eighteen-pounder guns; and he had never been in any doubt as to the nature of his job. Now that the detailed instructions had arrived, however, he had to be certain that he had them at his fingertips, for the penalties of bungling were too serious to ignore.

"Let's see," he thought. "When I sight the *Johanna*, I'll know her by a red flag with a white cross if it's day, or a white light at her fore and a red 'un at her mizzen if it's night. O.K. And she's to know me by

the same signs. O.K. And then I'm to board her, get
the goods—cigars, linen, and wine—and make back for
the river mouth. Then stick near the wharf at the
back of the tavern, and if there's an ordin'y light in
the bell-turret, keep off, but if it's blue, O.K. Well,
that's clear enough, isn't it? O.K."

While the captain mused over the coming adventure, a revenue officer in Baltimore was cogitating
over the same matter. He had long been suspicious
of the *Vision,* of York, Maryland, and lately his suspicions had so increased that he had issued his own
instructions to have her watched.

These suspicions were founded on a variety of
facts. One was that the *Vision* was an exceedingly
fast boat. She had been built, in fact, by the government, and had been used for chasing smuggling craft
in Pimlico Sound. Her draught had been too great,
however, so she had been sold at a public auction.
And subsequent inquiries suggested that the new
owner intended to turn the boat from a hound into
a hare.

Other facts colored this theory.

"What does she want with two eighteen-pounder
guns?" the revenue officer demanded of his second-
in-command. "You don't need guns for honest trade!"

"You need them for pirates," his subordinate pointed
out.

"Sure, you do," agreed the officer, "but I never heard
of a pirate plundering a boat for fish, and have we
any information that the *Vision* seeks or carries more
valuable freight? And what does she want with a

crew that size? And how does she pay for 'em?"

"Yes, that's what we've got to find out," nodded the second-in-command.

Another conversation was taking place at a tavern up a river mouth.

"Are those lights in the turret in order?" the proprietor asked the man. "Keep 'em clean—we'll be using 'em again soon, if we're lucky."

"If we're lucky," grunted the man.

"Why shouldn't we be lucky?" inquired the proprietor.

"This morning I passed a negress with a squint," replied the gloomy one.

That evening the *Vision* slipped quietly out into midstream and became a moving shadow in Chesapeake Bay. The revenue cruiser slipped out after her, and became a second moving shadow, while the servant in the tavern polished the glass of the turret-lamps. A third shadow was moving westward from the Atlantic Ocean.

If the captain of the *Vision* was cautious, so was

the officer in command of the revenue cruiser. He was in no hurry to overtake his quarry, which had to be caught with the evidence written large upon her, and he also had to be careful that the revenue boat was not recognized should her royals be sighted above the horizon line. The rig of the cruiser—a brigantine's— was familiar, and for camouflaging purposes the upper sails were kept furled until they were needed.

Much anxious time passed. Schedules could not be depended on in those days, and an expected merchant ship might be a week overdue. "Are we being followed?" wondered the captain. "Have they spotted us?" wondered the revenue officer. The answer in both cases was "Yes," and when at long last, near the end of the interminable bay, the revenue officer spotted a small boat making rapidly for the shore, he guessed that it had come from the *Vision,* changed his course, put on speed, and overhauled it.

The occupant of the boat seemed surprised at the interest taken in him. He was the pilot of the lighthouse, and he said he had just piloted the schooner out.

"A Baltimore boat," he added, "bound for Cuba."

"Ah—is that so?" queried the revenue officer.

"She's going to do coast-guard work there," nodded the pilot. "On her way now."

The revenue officer stared after the vanishing *Vision.* In a few moments it had vanished.

"Cuba's south," he frowned. "She's heading east."

"Oh, I can explain that," answered the pilot readily. "I heard the captain say he was sending some mes-

sage or other back by an incoming ship—no doubt
he's laying a course to meet her."

The officer's second-in-command observed:

"Well, if she's off for patrol work in Cuba, that'll
explain her guns and her crew."

"If," murmured the officer. . . .

The captain of the *Vision* was worried. He had
primed the pilot to tell his little fairy story, and the
pilot was a good friend of his; but that confounded
revenue fellow was hanging on as though he meant
it. For the moment, as the captain glanced back, he
saw a lovely empty space in his ship's wake. But now,
ahead, was another ship which he recognized from
signs to be the *Johanna*. What was going to happen
if the revenue cruiser came on? This unpleasant game
of follow-my-leader had begun in the dark, but there
was no darkness now to assist a poor smuggler to earn
a living! The daylight was pitiless!

The *Vision* had spotted the *Johanna*, and the
Johanna had spotted the *Vision*. "If that's not the
friend we're looking for," declared the *Johanna's* captain, "we've got no cigars and silk on board!" But
the next moment he changed his tune. His eyes
popped. "What's this?" he gulped. He was expecting a red flag with a white cross to be run up, but
instead up went the revenue flag of the United States!
What was worse, he was being ordered to lay to!

He had to obey. He could see the two long
eighteen-pounders, and he did not want a broadside.
It was tragic. Everything had gone so smoothly up
till then. . . .

"Hullo—what's this?"

His eyes popped again. The revenue flag was being run down, and another was being run up. A red flag with a white cross!

"Some funny business going on," he told himself. "This is my friend, sure. Keep your wits, now!"

As the ships established contact and the captain of the *Vision* stepped on board, the passengers and crew of the *Johanna* crowded to the side to discover what all the excitment was about. The captain of the *Vision* looked at the captain of the *Johanna* sternly, and accused him of having goods on board that were not on the manifest. He followed this accusation with the intimation that the goods would have to be handed over to him.

The captain of the *Johanna* protested with the expected indignation, but he followed his visitor to his cabin, and as soon as they were alone the visitor's attitude changed—as his flag had done.

"I'm the fellow you want to meet," he said quickly, showing his credentials, "but there's a real revenue boat after us that we neither of us want to meet. I've played this game to give you a story if the government man comes along and asks awkward questions."

"I see," answered the *Johanna's* skipper. "And now you want the stuff."

"Quick as gunpowder!"

"Well, I'm not stopping you!"

No goods were ever transferred from one ship to another more speedily. When the smart work had been accomplished, and the silks, cigars, linen, and

wine were safely stowed away in the *Vision*, the captain gave a receipt for the confiscated cargo—he gave
it with a wink—got back to his boat, and began showing his heels.

It was time enough, too. The revenue cruiser, the
commander of which had decided not to believe the
pilot's story, was now in view again, making for them
with all her canvas.

As the *Vision* began sailing away, the revenue
officer was presented with a pretty problem. Which
ship should he make for? Through his telescope he
had seen the conclusion of the transference, but he had
not been quite close enough to introduce the argument
of his guns.

While he hesitated, the *Johanna* hoisted her
distress-signal. The revenue officer's mind began to
spin. What the blazes did that mean? He answered
the signal, and continued on his course toward the
Johanna.

When close enough, he hailed her. "What's the
trouble?"

"Trouble?" the captain of the *Johanna* bellowed
back. He poured out a tale of woe, saying that he had
been robbed, and making the story as long as possible
in order to create delay. His object of course was to
give himself an alibi and the smuggling craft a good
start, but the revenue officer was not in a mood to
waste more time than he had to. After all that had
happened, he would look a fool if he returned to
Baltimore empty-handed.

"You see, you were wrong!" he snapped to his second-in-command, as the sails filled again. "Those two guns on board the *Vision* aren't for dealing with pirates—*they belong to pirates!*"

For that was his temporary interpretation of the incident.

The chase proceeded grimly. Each boat had a reputation for speed, and each strained now to justify it. There was no subtlety or bluff any longer, apart from such as could be introduced into the chase itself. Over a darkening sea, the law pursued the lawbreaker.

The weather-beaten captain of the *Vision* recalled, grimly, his comment on his final order: "This contract shall be in force one year from this day." He was keeping the revenue cruiser at a distance, and night was approaching to help him, but he could not continue this forever, and unless he thought of some ruse he had a very shrewd suspicion where he would be one year from this day!

Necessity is the mother of invention. The captain devised his ruse in the gloaming. When darkness was nearly complete, he swung round into the wind and made for Cape Henry. He was sailing without lights, and he prayed that the cruiser would have missed his maneuver and continue on. The two ships had started out as shadows, and now they were shadows again.

The captain breathed a sigh of relief. The pursuing shadow was being successfully duped. It continued on, before the wind, while the *Vision* struggled back toward Hampton Roads.

"We've won!" he chuckled, as he worked with compass and lead-line through the tricky shallows. "We'll double back to York before they——"

Crash!

The compass was faulty, and the lead-line had a kink in it, and the *Vision* never got back to York. She ended her career, with masts and rigging smashed, in an inconsiderate shoal.

The smugglers saved their skins by escaping from the sea's rage in small boats. But they did not escape from the law. In due course, in company with the captain of the *Johanna* and the untruthful pilot, they were brought to justice. The revenue officer may have failed to catch them, but he succeeded in giving evidence against them, and he did so with enthusiasm for the dance he had been led. . . .

"It seems to me," observed the proprietor of a tavern up a river mouth, "that we're not needing our light."

"Now p'r'aps you'll listen to me," grunted his man, "the next time I talk about a negress with a squint!"

A Date-Chart

1772. Case of a negro named Somerset, ending in the decision that a slave was free the moment he set foot on the British Isles.

1776. The first motion brought in the House of Commons condemning the trade.

1787. About this period "Abolition Societies" were started in America, and a committee with the same object was formed in England.

1788. Paris followed suit.

1791. Defeat of first Bill against further importation of slaves.

1792. House of Commons decided that the slave-trade should end on Jan. 1, 1796. House of Lords reversed the decision!

1794. America got busy and forbade American subjects to carry on the trade.

1807. United States banned importation of slaves from Africa. Abolition of the trade became law in Great Britain.

The Smuggler's Transition

THE FIRST Molasses Act had been unpopular enough. The second, which made the first
Act permanent, added insult to injury. A dozen years
were still to elapse before America sounded her
Declaration of Independence—a sound that still echoes
every July the Fourth—but wise men knew that in
the temper aroused by the second Molasses Act lay the
powder that would bring the ultimate explosion. Few
of the wise men were in Westminster.

In the best political tradition, the English government sugar-coated the new pill with a slight reduction
of the duty. But in its practical effects, this was a
distinction without a difference, and the sorely tried

American colonists refused to lick the sugar off. Smuggling continued with a vengeance, and the customs officers in many cases aided the smugglers' game. "What's the use?" they asked. Their sympathies, as well as their interests, lay with the smugglers. Sometimes, of course, the officials did their duty and brought defaulters into court; but, as in England, it was difficult to find juries who would return an adverse verdict, and many a smuggler got off free through the favor of his own kind.

The Molasses Act was followed by other detested legislation, and the Stamp Act in particular increased the rising heat. This latter injustice was repealed through the wisdom of Pitt, who put forward an argument in Westminster which, to the Americans, seemed long overdue—namely, that taxation and representation went hand in hand, and that it was an imposition to tax a man without a vote. The Act had already done its damage, however, and "Stamp Riots" were common in many towns, where stamped documents were seized and torn up or burned.

These incidents were bad enough, but it was the citizens of Provincetown who made one of the first really serious attacks on the dignity of England.

A British armed schooner, the *Gaspee*, was stationed in Narragansett Bay. Its mission of catching smugglers was unpopular, but Lieutenant Thomas Dudington, who commanded the ship, was more unpopular still. From all accounts he must have been what is termed "a nasty piece of work," and if the historians have overstressed his faults in order to justify the faults of his enemies, there is little doubt that he was tactless. Had he been a saint, America would not have loved him. As it was, his arrogance made a bad situation worse.

One day he ordered his ship to chase a smugglers' sloop. The rum-runner won the race, for the *Gaspee* ran aground at Namquit Point, which was afterward called Gaspee Point to commemorate the historic occasion. The sloop sailed back to Provincetown, carrying the good news of the British ship's dilemma.

Provincetown rejoiced, and saw a chance of rejoicing further. Why not complete what a beneficent shoal had begun? High tide would undo the excellent work unless it were circumvented by the higher tide of human feeling! So the drummers went forth to summon volunteers, and in a very short time enough men had answered the call to man eight boats. Muffling their oars, the eight boats slipped along the sea toward the grounded schooner, being joined en route by another boat from Bristol, the occupants of which were equally anxious to be in at the death.

It was a queer conflict. Nine little fish setting out to attack a wounded whale before nature, in the form of the rising tide, could effect its cure. If the wounded whale had not contained a Jonah in the form of the unpopular lieutenant it might have been left alone. The invaders were sighted just before they reached their victim, and the *Gaspee* gave them a broadside. The invaders came on. Maybe they were primed by the rum they were fighting for. They returned the fire, and a few minutes later it had become a hand-to-hand affair, with the attackers swarming up the schooner's side.

In the battle that followed, the lieutenant was slightly wounded. He and his crew were captured, bound, and sent ashore. From there they watched their ship burned over the tide that was rising to save it.

The attack had been conducted with impudent audacity, and the attackers boasted in the same spirit afterward. One of the men, Abraham Whipple, was so open in his boasting that the subsequent reward offered by the British government "for information" seemed pretty superfluous. Whipple was giving the information for nothing. But the form of his information was not, apparently, sufficient for the local authorities, who may have been meticulous in requiring sworn testimony that was not forthcoming. That the ringleaders were known is proved by the fact that a suggestion was advanced to send them to England for trial. A trial in America, before an American jury, would assumedly have been a mock one. The chief justice of Rhode Island refused, anyway, to sanction the suggestion, and after that a royal commission was appointed to investigate the matter. Nothing came of that, either. The British commander of the local naval forces, Captain James Wallace, could merely glare impotently at the defaulters, who grinned back at him. The grinner-in-chief was Mr. Abraham Whipple.

That such an incident could have occurred—the burning of a British ship—without normal redress, reveals quite clearly the condition of the times. When in due course the Revolution itself came along, Captain Wallace and Abraham Whipple, whose very name must have seemed like an insult to a man of sober dignity, had not forgotten each other. The captain sent a letter to his old antagonist, in which he declared:

"You, Abraham Whipple, on the 10th of June, 1772, burned His Majesty's vessel, the *Gaspee,* and I will hang you at the yardarm.—James Wallace."

To which came the Whipplish reply:

"To Sir James Wallace; Sir, Always catch a man before you hang him.—Abraham Whipple."

At the time of the *Gaspee* affair a number of men whose names were to become famous were pondering over the trend of events and preparing for it. Many heard the call before it was sounded. James Otis, John Adams, George Washington, Thomas Jefferson— these and others were alive to the imminence of the

coming ordeal and the probability of the new birth. The Molasses Acts, the Stamp Act—which had been passed to provide funds for maintaining an army to keep the colonists and the Indians in order—and many other pinpricks, had done ineradicable work.

Not long after the *Gaspee* affair, the angry American colonists threw down the gauntlet—in other words, they threw tea into Boston harbor—and from this damp beginning came the great flame out of which sprang their liberty. But when America became her own master, the smuggler felt a moral draught. He could no longer say, "I smuggle for my country—confound George III!" He had to say, "Confound Washington!" or Adams, or Jefferson, or Madison or whoever was the president of the moment. And that was not so easy.

Still, he managed it. When gold is the prize, people can manage most things, and the smuggler was certainly no exception to that rule. In fact, he managed it so well that, when his patriotic excuse was gone and the cloak of idealism had been wafted away from his bare skin, he threw himself into the business with added vim and flourished more greatly than ever! The only difference, apart from that of degree, was that now he robbed Uncle Sam instead of John Bull.

In other words, he became a smuggler impure and simple, and gave up trying to see an honest face in the looking glass.

He began with more excuse then his English cousin. He ended with less. The English smuggler was seeking in his own way to redress evils that had grown out of long traditional systems. England had had her experience, and was making a mess of it. But America was just beginning her experience —as her own ruler, at any rate. The smuggler did not even wait to give her a chance! Instead, he reaped a rich harvest out of the confusion of war's aftermath.

It was fortunate for the authorities that much of the American coast was impossible ground for smuggling, either because of its nature or its inaccessibility. The problem of land transport had to be considered by the smugglers after the contraband had been brought on shore, and they lacked the advantage of the English contrabandists, in whose smaller country "everywhere was near somewhere." Still, the American had a considerable length of coast to choose from, and if their conditions differed from those of the English contrabandist, their profits were just as great. Many retired, after a short career, to enjoy their doubtful earnings.

As in England, they had to be caught redhanded. They could not make swift journeys across the water as could the English smugglers of the southern counties; there was no convenient French coast opposite, and to them the Channel Isles were just a smugglers' dream; but they had countless friends among the captains of incoming merchant ships, and they set out from shore to interview them beyond the shore's horizon. The captains paused to say "How do you do?" and to pass their visitors something good; and then, while they resumed their journeys and reached port in the guise of respectable citizens, the smugglers slipped back to their shore, to conceal the contraband in warehouses especially built, or tunnels especially gouged, till they could transfer it to its final destination.

The captains of the big ships were just as smart at the game as their partners in the small ones. They concealed the goods that were not to be declared under other goods that were, or beneath fish, vegetables, or anything that bore an innocent look. One captain had a very useful hollow mast. A bumboatman came on board and tapped the contents. It was a common device for the merchant ship to sink goods with a buoy attached. In due course a little boat slipped out from shore and collected the buoy. Most of the American tricks were on a par with the English tricks, and if you can work out a good one for yourself, the odds are that some smuggler thought of it long before you.

There came a period when smuggling seemed on the wane. It is probable that, in the process of "finding herself," the United States was passing through an era when many of her citizens were also finding themselves, and taking an interest in obeying laws. It is equally probable that changing forms of transit had something to do with it. Preventive systems were certainly improving. But smuggling was not stamped out. It never will be, till the world learns to live without wars and rivalries and tariffs. And the wars in Mexico soon provided the smuggler with fresh opportunities for developing one of the least savory sides of his business.

In half a century Mexico had fifty-two different presidents or dictators or rulers—to say nothing of one emperor! One ruler was deposed, and another entered his place. One was popped off, and another popped up. Gun-running made many bad men's fortunes.

The Americans who smuggled war material into Mexico had no interest in Mexico's politics. They did not care whether this dictator rose to be shot at or that. All they cared about was their pockets, and they even went so far as to keep friction alive so that they might benefit by its stained results. If money is the root of all evil, the root could hardly extend to a greater depth!

There was some poetic justice in the strange weed which, a little later, these particular roots produced. In 1845 the United States got into a political tangle over the acquisition of Texas. It was actually a re-annexation, and the question of Texas' precise boundaries loomed suddenly into first importance. Boundaries that are fixed can be troublesome enough; when they are not fixed, they lead inevitably to conflict. Mexico had one idea on the subject, the United States had another, and as a result General Zachary Taylor and General Scott were sent south by the United States to seize the disputed territory. It took three years to bring Mexico to her knees, a fact which was not accomplished till many bloody battles had been fought and the city of Mexico had been captured; and one

reason why the Mexicans held out so long was because
they were equipped with guns and war material previously supplied to her by the United States smugglers!
American history has, perhaps, only supplied one more
cynical example of the boomerang.

The more cynical example came a few years later.
Smuggled war material had strengthened the division
between the United States and Mexico. Now smug-

gled slaves divided the United States against herself,
producing one of the bitterest conflicts in the story
of the world. Most of the northern states had already
emancipated their negroes, but in the South millions
of slaves still remained. The North wanted to free
these, as well. In the terrible struggle that followed,
smuggling dwindled to a negligible degree, saving
where it bore direct application to the war itself.

After the Civil War smuggling fell into the background as a matter of interest—waiting in the shadows for its most sensational spring! The smuggler needed something fresh to lift him into the real limelight again. He was destined to get it, in the next century, via Prohibition.

I own I am shocked at the purchase of slaves;
And fear those who buy them and sell them
    are knaves;
What I hear of their hardships, their tortures
    and groans;
Is almost enough to draw pity from stones.
I pity them greatly, but I must be mum,
For how could we do without sugar and rum?

WILLIAM COWPER

Tragedy in Black

THE NIGGER stood outside the hole of his hut. He was young, and the world seemed good. Cassava was plentiful, he had no disease, and not far off was a black girl, sitting under a big tree and grinning at him. Her grin made him feel gayer than the colors of the flashing birds. Suddenly she jumped up and ran away. He wondered whether it would be a good idea to chase her.

"No, too hot," he decided.

The heat was certainly oppressive. It came down from the sky and rose up from the ground. Much better stay still and be peaceful. He would chase her next time.

Then she came running back. She was no longer

grinning. There was terror in her eyes, and he stiffened. Others followed her, and in a few moments the forest clearing was filled with jostling, babbling people.

One fell dead.

The nigger guessed what the trouble was. There had been whisperings of late, especially at night when courage was low, and the oldest members of his tribe had been very gloomy, even including his father, who a few moons ago had killed a stranger and now wore his hat. It was said that weak tribes were being raided and taken from their homes, and that their own turn might come any moment. . . . Well, now it had come!

The nigger found himself running. Everybody else was running, and so, of course, he ran, too. He ran into two strong arms, and was lifted and swung against a tree. The world that had seemed so good, a short while back, became full of darting lights and pains. When he opened his eyes, he discovered that his hands were behind him, and he could not separate them because they were tied.

"All right, I'll just keep on lying here," he thought.

But someone kicked him, and he leaped up. He was kicked again, and he moved forward. He became one of a long black procession. Near him was a man wearing his father's hat. It was the man who had kicked him.

As he tramped he wondered what was going to happen to him. He supposed he would have to work for the conquering tribe, and be beaten when he didn't. He supposed he would not be free to run after the girl who had grinned at him. She would have to grin for somebody else. There was one thing he tried hard not to suppose. It was that they would be made "chop" of.

This, he knew, happened sometimes. There was an old man in his village who boasted that, in his youth, he had made "chop" of several enemies, which had not only satisfied his appetite but prevented the enemies from joining their ancestors. But, as a rule, raids were made for the charm of the women and the work of the men; or for priceless inanimate spoils such as hats.

Night came, and the procession halted. The nigger lay down, with seventy fellow captives, till dawn. Then the journey was resumed. In three days and three nights they came to a larger village than the nigger had ever seen. A second procession of captives arrived from another direction almost immediately afterward.

The chief of the large village came along and inspected them. He slapped them and prodded them. He looked anxious. So did the nigger, who felt from this inspection that they were certain to be made "chop" of.

But on the following day a long, flat boat came up the river by which the large village stood, and out of the boat stepped a short, thickset man in a complete suit. He was dark, though not quite as dark as the nigger, and he looked very funny. Impressive, too. Anybody who wore so many clothes, and such strange ones, must be Somebody. The white people the nig-

ger had heard about, but in whom he did not quite
believe, wore a lot of clothes. His father's hat had
once belonged to one of them.

And now the newcomer made an inspection. The
chief smiled at him and tried hard not to seem anxious,
but the newcomer was angry and prodded the prisoners viciously. He took hold of the nigger's thin arm,
seeming annoyed that it was not thicker, and that the
nigger was not in better condition.

But it was not the nigger's fault. He was tired,
and had not had much food during the long march,
and he knew he did not look nearly as well as when
he had stood outside his hut and the girl had grinned
at him. He did not feel as well. It was difficult to
feel well when the world was no longer good.

The newcomer and the chief had a long argument.
An old man by the nigger's side told him what it was
about. The chief wanted a little time to fatten them
up, and swore they would look a fine lot presently;
but the man in the complete suit said there was no
time for that, and he would have to take them as they
were or leave them. Then he started counting the
ones with ulcers. He threw up his hands. The chief
grew more and more depressed.

At last they disappeared into the chief's hut. When
they came out again, the chief was smiling. He had
had five ivory armlets when he had gone into the hut,
but he came out with seven. They reached down to
his wrist. He also had a magnificent hat, with a silk
handkerchief tied around it to protect it from the
weather.

The old man by the nigger's side glared sulkily at the chief. Once *he* had had eight armlets!

The captives were driven down to the river. More boats had arrived, and the nigger was bundled into one of them. Then began another journey. The nigger lost count of time. He longed to get out of the boat and stretch his legs, but no one was allowed to. Every now and then misery swept over him, and he joined in a dismal, moaning chorus. But he stopped when he was kicked or cuffed.

The banks of the river grew less steep, and the trees grew fewer. Low hills and swamps replaced thick forest. Creeks ran out of the river into muddy lagoons choked with mangroves. There was a smell of mud everywhere.

The nigger decided not to think. Not to worry. Just to lie as he was put, and sleep.

He awoke to a new sight. The boat had halted near the river mouth, and on the bank, standing in front of a large wooden building (the nigger had never seen so large a hut), were white men. He had never seen them before, either. He thought they looked horrible. Perhaps they wore all these clothes because they were ashamed of their pale bodies?

The leader of the white men—he was addressed as "Captain"—came to the water's edge and stared at the prisoners. He had a coarse, hairy face and small, cruel eyes. He seemed even angrier with the man who had brought them down the river than that man had been with the chief of the big village; and now this man was acting as the chief had done, pointing to the captives as though they were a splendid lot. In the middle of the wrangle another white man spoke to the captain, glancing anxiously toward the river mouth. The captain shrugged his shoulders and counted the captives. Then he turned to a number of tubs outside the wooden building.

One of the tubs was opened, and liquid came out of a hole. The nigger did not know, as the men drank, that this was the currency used for his sale, and that the vendor was testing it to make sure that it had not been watered. A hundred and fifty gallons of it purchased him, body and soul.

The bargain was struck. The nigger found his boat moving again. Fear seized him as the slave-supply station faded behind him and he saw the river mouth widening into a limitless expanse of water. He had never seen the sea before, or a boat of the size of that for which they were now making.

His companions began to moan. He joined them. The noise grew till it was impossible to hear the white men's swearing above the din. A whip descended on the nigger's bare back, and silenced him. Soon all was quiet again.

The little boat reached the enormous one. It was not really enormous, but it seemed so to the nigger, and when he stood upon its deck, with seven hundred others, he thought he was in a new world. Perhaps he had died in one of his sleeps, and had now been born again somewhere else!

He wore a loincloth. It was torn off. None of the blacks, whatever their age or sex, were allowed to wear anything, lest the filth in which they were destined to travel contaminate the material and increase the chances of disease. Naked, he waited, while small groups of thirty or so were detached from the main body and disappeared. He wondered where they went.

Presently his turn came. He moved off with a little band toward another part of the ship. He was made to stand opposite a burly man with a long thing that looked something like a pale snake. Now the burly man was pointing the snake at him. Swish! He leaped into the air, as salt water was pumped on him through a hose.

In time he would get used to this daily bath, but now he rebelled and ran amok. Three white men caught him, roaring with laughter. He hit one of them. The next moment he felt as though his head had been split, and his ears were filled with a loud singing. When he got over it, he found a weight on his feet. He was joined to the negro next to him by a small iron fetter.

After that, he gave up. The resignation of his race ate into him, and he submitted, without moving, to the extra douching he received.

Then came something a little better. A feed of meal. Concentrating on this temporary comfort, he did not notice that the boat had begun to move. Presently, however, the movement forced itself strangely upon his attention. It was not like any other movement he had ever known. A new terror took possession of him, entering his stomach, doing strange things to it, taking it away, putting it back again, pressing it up, shoving it down. He was sick.

And then, toward sundown, came the final misery

of the day. He was shoved down into his sleeping quarters.

The sleeping quarters comprised a long, low sweltering, swaying space. The length was about a hundred feet, the width under twenty. The roof was four and a half feet from the floor. Entering, the nigger had to stand, or stoop, until he received the order to lie down. The man who gave the order was a slave-packer. He packed the slaves, one against the other, as neatly as though they had been sardines. There was no discrimination between the sexes. The only point that mattered was the point of length. If short ones had been put against long ones, space would have been wasted, and there was not a cubic inch to spare.

Once more, the nigger could not move. He was one of seven hundred in the same predicament. He was sandwiched between a man and a girl; the man behind, the girl in front. The same girl who had grinned at him beneath a tree in the forgotten past.

So these seven hundred spent the night.

And so they spent night after night, for weeks. Thirty-four died where they lay; thirty from disease, the four from the results of flogging. The captain swore when he saw the casualties, for each death reduced his profit. The injury was to him. A dozen more developed ophthalmia and went blind. They were thrown overboard, for opthalmia is alarmingly catching, and the captain knew that once a crew had become completely sightless.

There was one time when the nigger thought he was going overboard, too. Not only him, but all the rest of the black cargo. It was a day of kicks and

shouts and bad tempers. Something was wrong somewhere, though he did not know what it was. They
had not been let out for their usual airing and hose-
bath, and the hose-bath had now become an occasion
to look forward to. If the salt water were violently
administered, at least it stirred sluggish blood after the
deadly, heated, packed hours of the night.

Shortly before sunset, a dozen of the negroes were
taken on deck. Our nigger watched them go with
apprehension, for there was a disconcerting grimness
about the man who had come to fetch them, and this
was an unusual time to leave their quarters below.
Soon a dozen more followed, and then a dozen more.
Where had they gone, and what was happening to
them? As the periodic departures continued, the anxiety of those who still remained increased.

Our nigger was in the final dozen. As he stumbled
up into the evening light, he beheld a startling spectacle.

All around the ship, on the very edge, were the
negroes who had preceded him. They were strung
to a long chain-cable, forming a living black necklace
round the boat. But it seemed they would not be
living for long. A heavy anchor, attached to the cable,
hung over the side. It was held to the side by a rope,
and a man stood by the rope with a large knife, ready
to sever it. At various points round the cable were
other men with knives. The nigger knew instinctively that, at a given signal, the knives would flash,
the anchor would descend with a great splash into the
slightly ruffled water, and the cable-chain would be
dragged down after it!

But he made no protest. His skull was numb. He was fastened to the death-chain as the others had been, and he awaited the fatal moment in a submissive stupor. He did not know why this was happening. He did not know whether it were a punishment, or the destiny for which they had originally been caught and sold. There were tribes who enjoyed watching death, though his was not one of them. Perhaps that was a pastime of the white men?

But all at once the captain, who had been staring at a speck on the horizon—a speck that had worried him all day, and that was now growing larger—raised his head and sniffed. Then he looked up at the clouds, and down at the water. He ran to the man by the anchor, and the man put his knife away. A wind sprang up and filled the flapping sails. The boat began to move more quickly, and to swing round on a new course.

Darkness fell. The wind increased. So did the pace of the boat. Spray splashed up, and drenched the necklace of negroes. When the sun rose, the negroes were all below again, packed together in their fuggy quarters.

"Why was all that?" wondered our nigger wearily. "Just to frighten us?"

He had no idea that the captain himself had been frightened, and that, if a sudden turn of the weather had not permitted the captain to escape from a government ship, he would have drowned between six and seven hundred negroes in preference to being caught redhanded.

And so the voyage went on. . . .

At the back of a little town in North Carolina, our nigger stood and waited with that patience which, by now, had become habitual. Whatever it was, you did what you were told. Life offered no alternative.

Presently he was shoved forward into a ring of people. A cardboard ticket flapped on his black chest. It bore the number "609."

"Now, here's a useful-looking brute," cried a little, dark-coated man with a hammer. "Did I hear someone say five hundred?"

"Six," called a voice.

"Six-fifty."

"Seventy-five."

"Seven hundred."

"Eight."

"Did you say eight hundred, sir?"

"Nine."

Thus, through bracelets and rum, our nigger at last found his commercial value in American dollars. He was knocked down for nine hundred and fifty.

The girl who had grinned at him and who, but for the white man's greed, might have made him a good wife, fetched a thousand.

From the New Bedford Shipping List,
December 3, 1861:

"In the U. S. Court in Boston on Friday,
Judge Clifford sentenced Samuel P. Skinner,
convicted of fitting out the Barque *Margaret
Scott* of New Bedford for the slave-trade, to
pay a fine of $1000 and to be confined at
hard labour for the term of five years in jail
at Taunton."

The sentence was too light.

The Amazing Lafitte

J E A N   L A F I T T E was the most famous smuggler in American history, and from the point of
view of romance and adventure he would probably
be selected as Smuggler Number One in a world-rank-
ing list. Complete books have been written about
him, he figures largely in all smuggling-literature of
comprehensive nature, and his latest bid to establish
himself on the permanent staff of immortals has been
through Hollywood. In *The Buccaneer* De Mille has
given him film fame—of a nature that would probably
astonish the debonair Jean himself if his ghost could
drop in at a cinema.

To begin with, the ghost might rub his eyes at the
title. "Buccaneer?" he would murmur. "Oh, this

must be about some other fellow! I wasn't a pirate!
Privateer—smuggler, sure, but not a pirate! Pirates
didn't like me any better than I liked them."

Then he would rub his eyes at his film version's
lack of knowledge on "Correct Behavior for a Gentleman." He would see himself taxed about wearing
too many rings. But if the wearing of more than one
ring was taboo by the best society in New Orleans at
the beginning of the nineteenth century, Jean would
have known it. He was not a follower of Society—
he was a leader of it. The assumption is that any
excess of jewelry would have been imitated, not cen-
sured. Jean Lafitte was the fashion.

His love affairs would also bewilder him, though
a fellow ghost, better versed in twentieth-century ways,
would quickly put him right on that score. "My dear
chap, this is a *film*," he would explain. "Do you suppose anybody would come to see you if there were no
love interest?"

"Perhaps it is because I am now, in a sense, a film
myself that I do not quite remember this love interest,"
Jean would retort. "And, *mon dieu*, I had certainly
hoped people would come to see me for myself alone!
But, *vraiment*, the love interest is very pretty. . . .
Only, tell me, where is my brother?"

"Oh—had you a brother?"

"Had I a brother! Do not let Pierre hear you ask
that! The reason Pierre is not with me is because he
was told he was not in the film, and I left the poor
fellow crying. I suppose they left him out because he
was crosseyed. Still, seeing that films do such won-

derful things—why, they make one of my sweethearts
go to war in a perfect-fitting uniform designed for
somebody else, and she comes through the battle with
her hair still in remarkable order—I should have
thought they could have straightened poor Pierre's
eyes. He is most terribly disappointed."

The film must not be blamed too greatly for its
inaccuracies. Probably there are plenty of inaccuracies
in other records of Jean Lafitte. The lily is always
gilded when a romantic figure rises to live in history
and when time has killed off the contemporaries who
might have checked the gilding.

Jean was born in 1780, in Bordeaux. We do not
hear much about his parents. He witnessed the French
Revolution through childish eyes, and doubtless the
example of adventure he found in France's agony
strengthened his own natural lust for it. When he
was fifteen he ran away. There were six other children and he may have thought they made enough
noise for one house. But his father thought differently,
went after him, and thwarted his intention of joining
the crew of a British man-of-war.

Jean ran away again. This time he evaded capture, and enlisted on the British frigate *Fox*. One of
the tragic anomalies of warfare is that, although there
is always some alleged ideal to justify the slaughter,
the people who do the slaughtering take little personal
interest in working out for themselves the rights
or wrongs of a particular issue! Thus armies are easily created for their thoughtless, devastating business.
Jean developed a "sense of honor" later, although this

was still open to criticism, and perhaps it could not be expected that a boy thirsting for sea thrills should care what flag he served under.

He soon tired of the *Fox*. After a few months he ran away again, but this time the operation was technically described as desertion. He found a temporary sanctuary with a French family living in Deptford, but he could not leave the wharves alone, and haunted them when big ships came from the west, bringing wonderful tales with their cargoes. Many of the tales were of the West Indies, and of the tempting troubles there. Jean could not sit passively until he had translated his newly fired imagination into reality—or exploded in the attempt.

He found a ship and went to Cartegena. This was a perfect district for his daring. The Spaniards had their grip on the local gold and were exploiting it for the glory of Spain; but the local folk who were being exploited by a stronger nation had begun to sit up and take notice. Rebellions and conflict ran through the Caribbean and the Gulf of Mexico like a flame. It was the old, old story, and Jean first touched the fringe of it, then went into the middle of it. He became a privateer—which is not ordinary piracy, but piracy legalized and authorized by a particular nation at war with the ships attacked—and adventures came to him thick and fast. So thick and fast, indeed, that it is impossible to extract the truth from the fiction. Owing to the number of tales told of Jean Lafitte, he himself, possessed of a keen sense of humor, never hesitated to add to them when the company and mood were ripe. He invented without the necessity, clouding the truth for the historian as well as for his contemporaries.

But it was not as a warlike individual that Jean Lafitte was first known in New Orleans. It was as a blacksmith. The Lafitte brothers—for Pierre joined him, though exactly how or when does not seem to be known to anybody—had their blacksmith shop in Bourbon Street, and all day long the hammers clanked and smoke belched from the forge in the little, low building opening onto the flagged sidewalks.

Jean and Pierre never did any of the work themselves. The workers were negroes, and it was soon noticed that the majority of the negroes appeared to have been taken on for short-term service, for they drifted mysteriously away, to be replaced by new ones. It was also noticed that wealthy plantation owners paid longer and more frequent visits to the blacksmith's than seemed strictly necessary for the shoeing of their mares.

But New Orleans did not mind. Louisiana was full of all sorts, and people did not make a habit of asking questions—particularly of the Lafittes, who were both popular in the town, and gave the most entertaining parties. If the bills for the parties were paid out of the profits of an illicit slave-trade, that was not the concern of those who enjoyed the parties. No one in New Orleans wanted, at that time, to bring an end to the careers of the slim, dark, fashionably dressed Jean and his more portly brother—despite the latter's squint.

As their secret trade grew and expanded, so did their social status. Jean was a connoisseur and an epicure, and he entertained freely. When others entertained, he was a welcome guest. A new shop was opened. Not a blacksmith's this time, but a shop where one could purchase wonderful silks and choice *objets d' art*—all at a very cheap figure. The shop was in Royal Street, a fashionable spot between Bienville Street and St. Louis Street, and all the Best People patronized it. The Lafittes were commercial as well as social assets.

Then came the crowning point of Jean's illegal activities. He was in touch now with slave-traders and privateers and smugglers and, through his business genius and his social connections, as well as through his great courage and sense of leadership, he was the recognized secret agent for the majority of contraband that drifted to the district. A headquarters of the smugglers with whom he now dealt was Barataria, with its two long sand islands, Grande Terre and Grande Isle. The islands are about six miles in length and two in breadth, and because they were difficult to reach they formed a perfect sanctuary for illicit activities. From New Orleans one had to reach them through vast swamps and a maze of creeks known only to very few.

Trouble broke out among the smugglers, many of whom were the lowest scum. They missed their opportunities through constant bickering and bloodshed, and no one was big enough to rise among them and take the reins. Although Jean Lafitte had had many

Jean Laffitte

SMUGGLER NO. ONE

dealings with the men, he had never visited their haunt. One day, smelling an opportunity with his unerring sixth sense, he paid them a visit.

At Barataria he became the iron man, though behind his firmness was glimpsed that quality which, in New Orleans, made him its most fashionable gentleman. It was this combination that singled him above his fellows. One assumes that even these unscrupulous ruffians could be influenced by the old school tie. Jean told them bluntly that they were fools to waste their blood, and that, as a business proposition, they were a washout. He coolly appointed himself as their leader, and before long he had established himself securely in that position. His headquarters existed now at both ends—among the riffraff of Barataria and the quality of Louisiana.

He was not accepted at Grande Terre until he had proved that he could be as firm in action as in speech. Among those who rebelled against his leadership was an ex-pirate named Grambo. An ugly scene was ended by Jean's bullet. It was Grambo's last rebellion on earth.

After this, there was no more trouble—of that particular sort. The original blacksmith's shop became a back number and was closed down. The new shop in Royal Street, fed by a now highly organized community at Barataria, prospered prodigiously and openly. Slaves who had once been passed on to their purchasers by secret processes were now openly auctioned, and bills advertising the sales were posted all over New Orleans. Till, at last, the newly appointed

Governor Claiborne decided that something must really be done about this impossible, law-defying dandy.

A revenue cutter was sent to deal with the Baratarians. The Baratarians received the officers with ironic courtesy, treated them to wine, made them drink to the Lafittes, and sent them away with instructions not to repeat the visit! The revenue cutter must have been sadly undermanned, or the officers themselves can hardly have deserved their title.

Further attempts having failed, Claiborne issued a proclamation in which he declared that the Baratarians were pirates, and warned the public against having anything to do with them. Very likely there were pirates among them, and certainly there were ex-pirates, but it is a fact that piracy was not included among the Lafittes' sins. They had enough without it. Their reply to what they may have regarded as impudence was greater impudence. They caused their "Sale of Slaves" bills to be posted next to the proclamation, and continued their fashionable social life.

Claiborne tried again. His difficulty was the same as the difficulty of dealing with smuggling in England. The public favored the smugglers, and offered no assistance to authority. He issued a second proclamation, ending as follows:

> I do solemnly caution all and singular the citizens of the State against giving any kind of succour to the said Jean Lafitte and his associates, but to be aiding and abetting in arresting him and them, and all others in like manner offending;

and do furthermore, in the name of the State, offer a reward of $500, which will be paid out of the treasury to any person delivering the said Jean Lafitte to the Sheriff of the Parish of New Orleans, or to any other Sheriff in the State, so that the said Jean Lafitte may be brought to justice.

This proclamation was issued and posted all over the city. Two results swiftly followed, the first tragic, the second comic. A constable tried to earn the five hundred dollars, and was shot. Then, two days later, another proclamation was found posted side by side with Governor Claiborne's. This was signed, not by Claiborne, but by Jean Lafitte, and it offered a reward of thrice five hundred dollars to the individual who would secure the Governor himself and deliver him to the smugglers at Grand Terre!

Only one man in New Orleans failed to enjoy the joke.

Claiborne's next step was an attempt to raise an army to attack the "Pirates"—for so he persistently called them. He applied to the state legislature for funds. This was an embarrassing request, since a number of the members of the state legislature had quite intimate dealings with Barataria, which explained why Claiborne was told, with apparent regret, that there were no funds to draw upon. Probably the Governor was in no doubt as to the truth of the explanation.

He kept on. The story of Jean Lafitte is largely the story of William Charles Cole Claiborne. He secured the arrest of Pierre, finding it easier to serve a warrant on the accessory than the principal. Pierre was not in the least worried. He took the warrant as smilingly as though it had been a birthday present. He even went to prison while awaiting his trial. When the trial came it proved a farce. Jean had retained the two cleverest lawyers in the district at a fee of twenty thousand dollars each. They were also the most unscrupulous, and Pierre walked out into the streets of New Orleans a free man.

The type of lawyers who secured Pierre's acquittal may be judged from the fact that one of them—John R. Grymes—relinquished his position as district attorney in order to accept Jean's bribe. He transferred his service from the state to the state's foe. The new district attorney fought a duel with him and received a bullet in his hip. Grymes then went to Barataria to receive his largess, and the small boat he went in sat much deeper in the water on its return journey. A week later he was as poor as a church mouse, having lost his fortune at cards.

Meanwhile, poor Claiborne continued to tear his long-suffering hair.

There is a glamour about the name of Jean Lafitte which it is difficult to retain when one comes down to most of the solid details of his life. He must have possessed an extraordinary charm, but he exploited his charm to very unworthy ends. It is with some relief, therefore, that we may now turn to an episode in his colorful career that does him greater credit.

In 1814 America was at war with England, and in the autumn of that year a British sloop of war, the

Sophia, appeared on the horizon of Grande Terre. As usual, the Baratarians were polite to distinguished visitors, and the Englishmen received a cordial welcome. Good food, good wine, and good stories led to an atmosphere of intimacyy, and the captain, sizing the smugglers up (as he imagined), introduced the real object of his visit.

"We are going to attack New Orleans," he told Jean, while they smoked cigars, "and we want you and your men to join us."

Jean adopted a noncommittal attitude. He wanted to hear more. The captain had more to relate. Half of it was in a letter from the commander of the British forces in Mexico—Captain Nichols—offering Jean Lafitte thirty thousand dollars, plus a commission in the British Navy, if he and his men would fight for them. The smugglers would all receive free pardons for any offenses already committed, together with His Majesty's protection. The other half was delivered verbally. "Refuse," said the captain, "and we shall destroy Grande Terre and hang every pirate who survives."

The English did not know the man they were dealing with. Thirty thousand dollars was nothing to him. He could make or lose that any night at gambling. He had paid forty thousand without winking to get his brother out of jail. And he was equally unimpressed by the second half of the message. To a man of his temperament, instead of being an urge to acceptance, it was an incentive to refusal.

But what the English knew least about Jean Lafitte

—and the Americans, too, for that matter—was his intense patriotism. He may have shown it in a peculiar way. He thumbed his nose at American laws and plagued the life out of American administrators. This was a very different matter, however, from joining an enemy from outside. Jean Lafitte, at this stage of his career, at any rate, was quite ready to lay down his life for his adopted country—provided, perhaps, that Governor Claiborne was not the person selected to make the request!

He did not rise and strike the British captain. He decided on subtlety. Adopting a this-is-so-sudden policy, he asked for ten days to think the matter over, and the captain, believing he had hooked his man, granted the request. As soon as he had gone, Jean dispatched a messenger to New Orleans, revealing the English plans, and sending the letter written by Captain Nichols. The news and the letter were accompanied by an offer to fight for the United States—for nothing.

It was then that Governor Claiborne made his worst mistake. It is difficult, after more than a hundred years, to estimate values correctly, to weigh contemporary evidence, and to judge impulses, but the sympathy one has felt for Claiborne up to this point switches over to Jean in what follows.

Claiborne decided that the news was false and the letter a forgery. He accepted neither the offer nor the advice. Instead of burying the hatchet and welcoming a substantial addition to his inadequate forces, he wasted valuable time and money in organizing an ex-

pedition against Lafitte himself, without giving any
indication that he was going to do so.

Seventy men, under Commodore Patterson and
Colonel Ross, left New Orleans in three barges.
Twenty-four hours down the broad Mississippi the
barges were met by the armed schooner *Carolina,* and
on the following day, near the river's mouth, they
were joined by half a dozen small gunboats.

What happened when this formidable fleet appeared in Barataria Bay?   Perhaps we shall never
know exactly, since versions differ, and those who recorded the surprising events at the time generally had
some personal ax to grind. But the student of history
will probably eliminate certain details portrayed in the
film, which shows gunfire from the American ships
creating havoc among the astonished Baratarians, who
imagined the Americans were their allies. Actually,
it appears, not a single shot was fired.

The following seems to have been the course of
events.

Spotting the smugglers' boats in the harbor, Patterson hoisted a signal flag on the *Carolina,* "Clear for
action." He did not show the nationality of his fleet,
and Lafitte believed, with justification, that it might
be the English who had arrived to carry out the threat
of extermination. He closed the harbor mouth with
a line of ten vessels, and prepared to give the "English" the warmest possible reception.

Then Patterson hoisted the American flag. Jean
stared in astonishment. If the ships were American,
why had they prepared for action? He realized then

that these Americans were as big a menace as the English would have been, but he could not treat them in the same manner. He altered his plans, and very shortly Patterson saw another American flag ascend at the fort, together with a white flag.

Being set for a scrap, Patterson may have experienced a twinge of disappointment; but he could not ignore the white flag, and his own next move in this queer bloodless battle was to hoist a flag of truce. The matter seemed to be all over bar the shouting.

Smoke rose skyward from two of the largest vessels in the harbor. As the smoke went up, the flag of truce came down. Patterson angrily gave the signal for battle, and his boats advanced to attack. The trouble was that they received no opposition, saving from the shallowness of the channel, which grounded two of the gunboats. When the rest got by they found the smugglers in flight.

Swallowing his wounded pride, and refusing to be captured, Jean Lafitte preferred to run away rather than to fire on an American ship.

Not all the men got away. Patterson caught nearly a hundred of them. He also captured half a dozen undamaged ships, and contraband to the value of a hundred thousand pounds. It was, materially, a good day's work, whatever its other aspects. Somewhat ironically, after Patterson had left, the English ships turned up, but found neither friend nor foe to greet them.

Jean and his men—he still had five hundred by him—found a temporary sanctuary at a spot called

Last Island, and they remained hidden there while matters developed swiftly and alarmingly at New Orleans.

The threat of invasion became more and more acute, and the citizens struggled not to develop panic. Jean Lafitte and his five hundred men were available to help the city, but Jean was biding his time, and knew that he would not be welcomed until the eleventh hour. General Jackson, in whose hands lay the security of New Orleans, refused to traffic with pirates or smugglers, and he even issued a proclamation in which he made his objections clear.

Meanwhile the British menace grew and grew, and presently news came that from twelve to fifteen thousand British soldiers had left Ireland for New Orleans. They were formidable men, for they were freed from the valuable experience of the Napoleonic Wars, now concluded.

Jackson's face became grim. He found fear and apathy all round him. There seemed little hope that New Orleans would withstand the coming onslaught which had been approaching so gradually but so surely. He needed reinforcements. General Coffee, in an historic march which forms a story in itself, was bringing more men from the north, but the British were winning the tortuous race. It appeared impossible that General Coffee could reach New Orleans in time to save it.

Then Jean Lafitte took the initiative. During his period in hiding he had continued with his trade and accumulated his possessions. Men were wanted. He had five hundred of them. Ammunition was wanted. He had quantities of it, concealed in a cache on his island. He also had 7500 flints for flintlock muskets. And suddenly he appeared in the streets of New Orleans where he had been so familiar a figure in the past, and walked into the headquarters of General Jackson, in Royal Street.

It was the first time they had met. Each man was a master of his particular craft, and a born leader of his particular followers. They sized each other up quickly.

"I have offered before to put my forces at the disposal of the government of the United States," said Jean bluntly. "I offer them again. My men, my ships, my ammunition."

Jackson nodded, and replied as bluntly:

"We accept your offer. It is timely, and the United States is grateful."

Thus, without frills, but possibly with a little inner wince, General Jackson accepted help from the "hellish *banditti*"!

Governor Claiborne may have winced, too. His feud with the distracting smugglers had been of longer duration. But he, like the general, yielded to the necessities of the time, and he issued a proclamation which must have astonished the ghosts of many previous proclamations he had signed. It ran:

> The Governor of Louisiana informed that many Individuals, who may be, or are supposed to be implicated in the offences hitherto committed against the United States at Bara-

taria have for some time past concealed themselves
on account of their inability to procure Bail, in
case of an arrest, but who at the present Crisis,
manifest a willingness to enroll themselves and to
march against the Enemy, he does hereby invite
them to join the Standards of the United States,
and he is authorized to say, should their conduct
in the Field meet the approbation of Major-Gen-
eral Jackson, that officer will unite with the Governor in a request to the President of the United
States to extend to each and every Individual as
aforesaid so marching and acting a Free and Full
pardon.

New Orleans was saved, and largely through the
conduct in the field of the Lafitte brothers and their
strange assortment of men. But Jean never regained
his place in New Orleans society. The old tradition
had been snapped. The new was not wiped out by his
heroism in battle. When introduced to General Coffee
at a great ball, he noticed the general's momentary
reaction to the name. It was not complimentary. Extending his hand, Jean said, "Yes—Lafitte, the pirate."
The general smiled and took the hand.

A few days later, however, the Lafitte brothers
vanished from New Orleans—almost as mysteriously
as they had arrived. They went out in the void, doubtless drawn by the mysterious beckoning of adventure.
Over the adventures themselves is drawn a veil.

But one is grimly sensed, if a report in an old,
preserved Baltimore newspaper speaks truly, and those
to whom the name of Lafitte stands for romance and

magic read it with a little sigh. The date is 1826, and the report runs:

Lafitte, the Noted Pirate, Killed. A British sloop of war fell in with and captured a piratical vessel with a crew of sixty men, under the command of the famous Lafitte. He hoisted the bloody flag and refused quarter and fought until nearly every man was killed or wounded—Lafitte being among the former.

Which Lafitte?

To Prohibition's Ashes

When Uncle Sam said, "We'll go dry,"
Crooks ceased to mourn the days gone by,
And tossed their hats into the sky
When Uncle Sam said, "We'll go dry."

He meant it well, did Uncle Sam,
But soon the Eastern epigram
That runs, O *Watanasiam*,
Came to the mind of Uncle Sam.

From every source the liquor poured
As Law went splashing overboard.
The conscience sank, the drink-bill soared,
And what could not be drunk was stored.

Then Uncle Sam said, "We'll go wet!"
The crooks turned pale and begged, "Not yet!"
Their goose was dead; their sun had set,
When Uncle Sam said, "We'll go wet!"

Prohibition and All That

NO HISTORY of smuggling would be complete without a chapter on American Prohibition, but no chapter on American Prohibition could do more than touch the fringe of that amazing and exhaustive subject. Probably we are still too close to it to be able to judge it in enduring terms. We call it, variously, a disastrous experiment, a glorious failure, an impossible attempt to reach the stars, a study in ethical fanaticism. The one certain thing is that, in its immediate effects, Prohibition produced cynically grotesque results, increased the evil it attempted to end, and introduced many others.

Whatever may be one's personal views on the subject of drink and its value or otherwise to an individual and a nation, it is depressing to realize that no politicians have ever won over the millions to a purely moral cause, yet at any moment they may urge those millions to limitless sacrifice, bloodshed and slaughter for so-called peace. Patriotism will induce people to drop bombs on one another's heads and thrust bayonets into one another's stomachs, but it will not hold them from their glass of liquor, or from cheating their government or one another for the sake of personal profit.

We live in a queer world, and our right to criticize others generally dissolves in our own participation in the queerness.

Prohibition was intended to make America more moral, more healthy, and more efficient. It did none of these things. Morality sank to some of its lowest levels, health suffered through the fearful liquor that was poured down millions of American throats, and the only increase in efficiency was displayed by human ingenuity in evading the law. In that sense, undoubtedly, efficiency was produced. The amateur law-breaker and the professional criminal became greater experts than ever before.

At first—for a short while—it was the small man's game. The ordinary smuggler, who had been going through rather a thin time, raised his nose and sniffed. Hello! Here was something good! Stop drink? *Drink*? Say, who's the fool? Come on in!

Using all his old devices, he turned his full attention to the most popular of all contraband, and his easily found customers grew and grew and grew. They grew so extensively that they attracted the attention of the big man—of the man who thought not in little figures but in large ones. The small man was "frozen out," or became the servant of the big man, who brought arms into the business and carried guns.

America had two hip pockets. One for a flask, the other for a revolver.

And then the mental and moral demoralization set in, and conscience began to rot. Authority was derided as, perhaps, it had never been derided before, and because one law was broken with impunity, others collapsed as well. It was a case of everybody doing it. If anyone wanted to justify himself, he only had to turn his head and see his neighbor.

The old smuggling gangs of Kent and Sussex found their modern counterpart in Chicago and every big city. Every kind of criminal entered the game, and it was a game without sportsmanship. If the small man wouldn't play it the big man's way, he was kicked out of the way. If the big man found a rival on "his territory," his boys called upon the enemy and took him for a ride. Prohibition brought fame to such men as Al Capone, Jack (Legs) Diamond and Machine-gun Kelly. Money makes money in bad business as well as good, and the millionaire bootleggers amassed so much of it that they could purchase officials in addition to thugs; and, since the officials enjoyed their drink as much as the thugs did, the crooked path was rendered all the easier to travel.

At one end, the arch-crook; at the other end, the bright young thing. At one end, murder; at the other, mirth. It was a long chain extending from sinister darkness into false light, and all the links of the chain were faulty or stained.

And the irony of the situation was that it was forced upon the unwilling community by idealists. Men like "Pussyfoot" Johnson, who smiled with commendable courage through their own personal damage, believed in wings before their time.

Of course all the American officials could not be purchased. There were many splendid men who, whether they agreed with the law or not, made strenuous efforts to see that it was carried out. They fought against heavy odds, found their own friends in the opposite camp, but struggled desperately on. The annual expense bill for fighting the bootlegger rose rapidly to seven million dollars. The man in the street paid the bill, but he gave little assistance to get his value. He preferred to get his glass. So the cost of the glass went up while the quality of what went inside it went down.

The smugglers' fast motorboats slipped out from countless points in America's long shore, from Maine and Massachusetts down to Florida, transshipped bottles and barrels from larger boats beyond the territorial limit, and then slipped back again. At one time it was estimated that only one boat in a hundred was captured—and, if an American cynic is to be believed,

"that by mistake." Often the smugglers' motorboats fled back south, to some lonely swiftly organized center well out of the American eagle's eye, bringing the stuff north again by means of modern rapid transit which the smuggler of old would have given his apology of a soul for.

Most people did not trouble to find excuses for themselves. The art of thinking declined. But some of those who attempted mild defenses hit upon very odd ones. Here is some reasoning by an Englishman, James Barbican, who has written a racy volume describing his rum-running experiences. The book came

out while Prohibittion was still in being, and in its
final chapter he says:

> The Americans as a nation are determined to
> have "hard liquor," and when they can't get the
> real thing they poison themselves with evil sub-
> stitutes which they kid themselves into believing
> came "straight from the ship," or "from the cellar
> of a man who is selling up his pre-prohibition
> stock." . . .
> So who can blame an Englishman for joining
> in a game which provides the American nation
> with good liquor instead of bad, and himself with
> adventure and profit?

The last half-dozen words in this defense are elo-
quent. Without them, would we have had this Good
Samaritan? But Mr. Barbican writes with a genuine-
ness that disarms criticism, and he evidently thought
his excuse good enough. Incidentally coming from
one who knew a great deal about the game, his picture
of the effect of Prohibition on American health is a
pretty grim one.

Passengers traveling to the United States, whether
American or English, made it a practice to drink roy-
ally up to the twelve-mile limit, beyond which their
wine bottles were legally taboo. This gave an impetus
to the wine that was brought on board, and a considerable amount of it got beyond the twelve-mile
limit, as was intended from the first. The game was
carried on by crews as well as passengers, and—as an
example—an American sailor, a member of the crew

of the *City of Alton*, was fined thirty-eight pounds at West Hartlepool for trying to smuggle across thirty-five bottles of whisky "intended for personal use during the voyage." Unfortunately for the sailor, the rummaging officers did not believe that the whisky so much as the profits therefrom were intended for personal use, especially as the bottles were carefully concealed under a floor. "Why hide it?" they inquired. "From the captain," answered the sailor. "If he'd known, he'd have taken it away." The officers took it away instead, and charged over a pound a bottle for the cartage.

The twelve-mile limit was arrived at in a rather unorthodox manner, after a little international breeze. By the ordinary rules American territory ended three miles from shore, which meant that they had no right to search ships beyond that range. This presented a difficulty, since smuggling craft could establish contact with unsearched ships too near to the coast, and only had a three-mile run to get home with the goods afterward. So American lawyers got busy, and dug up some old precedent which, they alleged, permitted America to search all ships as soon as they were twelve miles away.

This added nine miles to American territory, and the English captains who imagined themselves immune in these waters were mightily indignant to find American officers boarding their ships. They submitted at first. When crews were arrested and liquor confiscated, however, they complained to their government, and the British government in turn complained to the American government, denying the new twelve-mile-limit rule most emphatically.

America gave way. She really had no legal leg to stand on. But some good came out of it for her, as the little breeze led to an arrangement by which England permitted her ships to be searched twelve miles from the American coast in return for the privilege of being allowed to carry sealed liquor.

When Prohibition ended, American law began to breathe again. The fat-pocketed gangsters wept and gave farewell parties to their greatness. The most amazing, the most brazen and the most swiftly demoralizing smuggling in history had come and gone.

But smuggling did not end. It merely decreased and changed its character. If liquor was no longer forbidden, there were still duties to pay on it, as upon countless other articles involved in the mad race of international trade war; and smuggling is going on steadily at this moment. Otherwise, thirteen hundred American inspectors would not be doing whole-time duty against the modern bootlegger.

If you want to visit one of smuggling's most prosperous centers today, go to the French islands of St. Pierre and Miquelon, south of Newfoundland. You will see nothing, on the face of these isles, to indicate the source of their prosperity. You will find countless honest men there who pay their taxes and go to church, and who perhaps dislike smuggling more than you do. "This is a cod-fishing district," they will tell you. And that it will be true.

But cod-fishing did not build the two big breakwaters that guard the inner harbor of tiny St. Pierre against the winter storms, or keep the great dredger continually at work, or develop the prosperity of the cafés. St. Pierre has a total length of four miles, but it boasts of luxurious motorcars and a taxi-rank.

Three hundred years ago the islands were a convict settlement. After the convicts departed, fishing kept the native folk alive. Then came Prohibition and the grand transformation. French territory—an adjacent Canadian coast—and the waiting American shore— these formed a perfect combination for work that was afoot! The convicts had gone, but rascals as great now visited little St. Pierre, which puffed itself out like the frog till, surely, it would burst! Fishermen, beachcombers, rolling stones, strangers all began to congregate. Lone hands grew into small groups, and the small groups were swallowed up by syndicates. The syndicates apparently carried on legal businesses, and opened the most innocent-looking offices. But the business carried on behind the office doors was the smuggling business, and the business still flourishes.

The prizes of smuggling are very tempting. Since religion teaches us that we are all miserable sinners, it is not surprising that the practice still goes on. It will continue to go on till we cease to be sinners, or till the material reward of sinning grows less. The first solution is in the hands of the moralists, the second in the hands of the politicians. If the politicians do not improve in their job, will the moralists come forward again to take a hand? After Prohibition, will they dare?

Perhaps, after all, smuggling—like everything else —is just a personal question.

Reported by the British United Press, April 6, 1937:

"Fifty passengers from the 20,000-ton Hamburg American liner *Reliance*, which is on a world cruise, watched the execution of six drug-pedlars in Pekin to-day.

"They were on a sight-seeing trip to the Temple of Heaven when they saw soldiers march six men into the grounds and force them to kneel against a wall.

"Then the soldiers drew revolvers and shot the condemned men in the back of the head from a few inches away."

Smuggling Up to Date

THE SMUGGLER of today is a very different proposition from the smuggler of yesterday.
Ask any artist to draw you a smuggler of the eighteenth century, and he will give you a recognizable
outline or silhouette in sixty seconds; but ask him to
draw you a smuggler of the twentieth century, and
he will be stumped.

For the modern smugglers have no recognizable
guise, saving perhaps to the experienced customs officer who has an instinct for them as a dog has for a
bone. The smuggler of the 1930's may be a fashionably dressed lady (and frequently is), or an innocent-
looking gentleman in a top hat, or a nursemaid, or a
tough, or a Bright Young Thing at a holiday hotel,

racing round the Isle of Wight in a speedboat. Put a hardened modern smuggler among half a dozen respecters of the law at an identity parade, and you will never be able to pick him—or her—out!

Smuggling used to be largely a matter of brawn. Now it is mainly a matter of brain. Sometimes the brain is devilishly clever. Sometimes it is amazingly silly. Possibly one traveler out of every ten who read these words will have had a shot at smuggling, and will have his own personal story-bag of successes or failures. The successes far exceed the failures, and many small shopkeepers will tell you, if you get them in a confidential mood and if they spot you as either a "sport who can keep a secret"—or better—as a potential customer, that in these hard times they could never keep alive but for certain useful, regular callers who keep them provided with tobacco, cigarettes on which no duty has been paid, and pornographic literature. You can leave their shops yourself, if you like, with amazing bargains, and return home to smoke cheap cigarettes while looking at even cheaper pictures. All you have to do is to decide that it is quite legitimate to cheat your own government, and to accompany the shopman into his back parlor. Perfectly simple, if you don't mind that sort of thing. Moreover, with that facile logic by which it is human to justify all one does, you can tell yourself that you are only helping to keep a poor bloke alive or save him from becoming a burden on the rates.

But although the successes exceed the failures, the failures are costly when they occur, and if you are thinking of your own security it will be safer to profit by somebody else's smuggling than by your own, even though the profit, should it accrue, will not be so great.

As a warning to the too venturesome, here is a handful of recent failures, which provide typical examples of what happens when the venture does not come off.

A Hendon lady tried to evade payment of duty, at Dover, on a white ermine coat and a couple of silk nightdresses. Probably it never occurred to her that she was doing anything really wrong, for it is amazing how many people regard smuggling as legitimate; but when she found herself being questioned more closely than she either liked or expected, she—in her own subsequent words—"lost her head and told an untrue story on the spur of the moment." She admitted this was silly, and she apologized, but the silliness cost her a fine of £50, plus a sum of £250 (representing thrice the value of the articles and the duty on them), plus five guineas costs. Net result, for bringing into England clothes worth £60, she had to pay an additional £305 5s.

A traveler returned from South Africa with a bag of golf clubs among his baggage. All the baggage, barring the golf bag, was delivered across the counter, but the golf bag remained clutched in the owner's hands. But for this, the customs officer might not have troubled to examine the bag, and the traveler cursed himself afterward. It is disconcerting, however, how differently a scene that has been pleasantly imagined works out in reality, and many a novice has been caught at the crucial moment by sudden doubts and flurry. In the bottom of the golf bag were gold watches, the duty on which amounted to over a hundred pounds. The hundred pounds was a mere moiety of what the man had eventually to pay.

Two aviators used the air for the free transit of brandy and cigars. Something went wrong with the air, and they had to appear at the Folkestone police court. One was fined £100 and £25 costs, the other was fined £200 and £50 costs.

These fines, unpleasant though they were to those who had to pay them, pale into nothingness compared with a fine imposed in 1934. A gang of tobacco-smugglers was tripped up, and their activities interested the court for a considerable time. The little price the gang eventually had to pay for past offenses amounted to £30,000!

These are merely a few typical smugglers' tragedies, of a kind that occur regularly every year. Sometimes the tragedies reach those who, not smugglers themselves, make use of the fraternity, either knowingly or by the convenient process of "closing an eye," which is a distinction without a difference. It was claimed by one man in a recent case that he did not know whether a consignment of whisky that came into his hands was contraband or not, but the court refused to believe him, and the evidence certainly supported the court's skepticism. As he could not pay the fine, he went to prison for three months and lost a lucrative job.

That, of course, is one side of the picture. It is easily the smaller side.

The amount of duty "saved" annually by the revenue men is less than a quarter of a million. In the year ending March 31, 1936, there were 8523 seizures. But while the amount of duty which is not saved, and of which the country is cheated, cannot be determined with any certainty, this figure is probably around about eleven or twelve millions, when one includes both professional and nonprofessional smuggling. This means that the smuggler loses under one-fortieth of what he tries to get away with.

The authorities are doing all they can to stem the rising tide—it has been rising pretty steadily since 1932 —and they are increasing the fines and the penalties. It is not generally known that there is a special Investigation Branch of the Customs and Excise Department, the object of which is not the collection of dues, but the collection of those who try to dodge them. This Secret Service works well and enthusiastically, and has proved its value since its institution; but it is up against a most perplexing proposition, and in spite of its efforts the smugglers continue to expand and prosper.

Politics, of course, are all in their favor. High tariffs are the food they fatten on. Free trade is their dread and their bugbear!

The offices of the Customs Investigation Department—a second C.I.D.—are in Lower Thames Street, where specially selected men devise means and gather information for tripping the smuggler up. Probably no little band of men has ever had to tackle so elusive an army! A scout gives them some news that leads to the raiding of a night club. Another overhears and repeats a scrap of conversation that takes a C.I.D. man into a dingy shop in the East End, where the smile gradually fades from the good-natured shopman who receives him. A telephone call necessitates an urgent trip to some lonely shore or creek. A trivial incident, reported by a smart customs officer, may direct embarrassing attention to the books of some big city firm, or to some hitherto unsuspected character.

The character is as likely to be a woman as a man, for women are particularly ingenious—and unscrupulous—in their methods. They are unscrupulous when they bank on man's chivalry and conceal goods next their skin. They are apt to forget that female officials may look where males fear to tread! One young lady who had to be stripped was suspected by her sprightly walk. Surely, thought the officials, no woman could possess such a brisk gait when overburdened by such vast amounts of superfluous flesh? The superfluous flesh proved to be undeclared silk swathed round and round the too nimble body. The young lady was clever, but not quite clever enough.

Another long-skirted lady seemed to be having trouble with her garters. A rude official sent her into a private room to take off her skirt and reveal the cause of her difficulty. The difficulty proved to be half a dozen long, pencil-shaped cases fixed round the garter, and containing dope.

It was a woman, too, who stepped ashore one day

with a cat and several kittens. She was carrying them in a basket, and they were evidently not very good sailors, for she was trying to console them with words of comfort. A customs officer with a soft heart stepped forward to add his spot of comfort and stroked the cat. The cat was quite unresponsive. As a matter of fact, it was past caring about anything at all, for it was stuffed. So were the kittens. Their posthumous contents included two thousand pounds' worth of drugs.

Hiding places being used today are endless. Horse collars, statuettes, soap, umbrellas and walking sticks, heels of shoes, fake cameras, tubs of flour, onions— these are random selections from a list yards long. Who would be a customs official, when every person met and every article encountered is suspect? Infinite tact, as well as infinite intelligence, is necessary to hold the thankless job. Even cork legs and glass eyes have been used for carrying contraband. The smuggler applies no limit to his methods.

One of his methods is to be on the constant lookout for accomplices who, while possessing the means of affording assistance, will be the type of person least likely to be suspected. These accomplices frequently have to be changed. They lose their nerve, or their interest, or they are caught. They are rather indignant when they are caught, because they will often tell you that they have only entered into the game for the sport of the thing. Born into a world that is struggling against severe odds to retain its simple, ethical sense, that is confused by laws and restrictions and politics, that is often rendered cynical by the strange course of events, and that is sometimes undermined by the very pace of existence, they lack the resistance of a former generation to ephemeral temptation. Life, to these people, must have its thrills, and when one thrill has been exhausted, they search round for another.

The smuggler who makes a serious business of his calling is as keen a judge of character as is the customs officer who tries to catch him. He studies psychology as well as geography, and he is a shrewd student of a situation. He watches Algy in his speedboat. Notes the risks he takes. Estimates the brain, or lack of it, behind the cackling laugh. Hears him boasting at the hotel bar. And, choosing the right moment, tackles him one day.

"That's a smart little boat of yours," he observes, "and you know how to handle her."

"Oh, nothin' to it," replies Algy airily. "She's a bird. Handles herself."

"She wouldn't if I were her skipper," answers the smuggler. He does not look like a smuggler. He looks like an ordinary businessman, which is what Algy takes him for. "But don't you get bored, just going round and round?"

"Oh, I don't know," muses Algy. "It's a big splash, wherever you go."

"It would be a bigger splash, if you had some particular point to go to," responds the smuggler. "That's what *I* should want if I were in your shoes—and if I had your boat and your skill."

"Don't think me impertinent and so forth, old

fruit," says Algy, "but *what* are you talkin' about?"

"Have a cigar," suggests the smuggler, "and tell me what you think of it. If you like the brand—and you will—I can get you a box."

"What do they cost?"

"To a smart fellow with a speedboat—nothing."

Algy finds the cigar excellent. While he smokes it, the conversation continues. Afterward, he returns to his hotel thoughtfully, with two more cigars in his pocket. One for himself and one for a friend.

The friend motors from London every week end. He is never really happy until the pointer has got just beyond the eighty. Then life begins.

"Have a cigar," says Algy that night, "and tell me if you like it."

His friend does like it.

"Like to be supplied with 'em for nothing, old top?" inquiries Algy.

"Let's hear the low-down," replies his friend.

Algy gives him the low-down. His friend grins.

"Well, what's happenin' in the little brain-pan?" asks Algy.

"Quite a lot," answers his friend. "In fact, it's a riot!"

"Some fun," murmurs Algy.

A few days later, Algy does not go round and round in his speedboat. He goes out and out. Though when he reaches a certain motor launch that left the French coast that morning, he returns to his encircling movements. When he is close, and right under the motor launch, something comes down to him at the end of a rope. A safe landing effected, the rope is released. A heavy tarpaulin is spread over the new cargo, and Algy speeds back to the home shore.

"Good hunting?" asks his friend, arriving from London that night.

"I harpooned a whale," grins Algy. "Do you think you could tow it back to town tomorrow night?"

The "whale" is towed back to town at eighty miles per hour.

So much for Algy, and so much for his friend. After putting the car to bed in a private garage, his friend keeps away from the garage for twenty-four hours. During those twenty-four hours, our smuggler, armed with a duplicate key, visits the garage and removes the "whale." In other words, a large consignment of cigars on which no duty has been paid.

He keeps a box or two for himself and spends the next few days visiting shops. In some he is known. Without any preamble, he is invited into the back parlor, and a transaction takes place. But in others he is a stranger. He is always breaking new ground, for you never know when the old ground will turn sour. Besides, business is expanding.

"Have you got a good, cheap cigar?" he inquires, in one of the new shops.

The shopman, behindhand with his rent, produces a box eagerly. His customer tries one, sniffs it, and asks the price. The shopman informs him.

"Sorry," says the customer. "I asked for a *cheap* cigar, and good!"

The shopman looks pained and assures him he will not find a better, cheaper cigar in London.

"I've got a better, cheaper one in my pocket," retorts the customer, and produces it. "If you stocked *this* brand, you could make a small fortune."

The tobacconist examines the cigar, inquires the price, and is amazed. He asks where he can get them at that figure. "From me," replies the customer. "How about a little chat on the subject?"

And thus the humble tobacconist is drawn into the net. He may be a man who has no moral scruples, or he may be a man who, urged by his own personal troubles, easily yields to a simple temptation. In either case, he becomes a party to the great fraud, and before long he has tipped the wink to a selection of confidential customers, who form the other end of the long chain.

Before long, too, he is out of debt.

The shopman, once on the downward path, has an additional way of adding to his profit, should he want to. It is an odd fact that, if a customer is not an expert, he is even easier to deceive than the customs officials themselves. The very word "smuggled" is apt to give him inflated ideas of value, and if he is cleverly handled he may be duped into believing that an inferior article is "something special," simply because it is contraband! Thus a cigar on which no duty has been paid may be sold at above its normal figure. The same applies to many other contraband articles, such as perfume, powder and liquor.

If only some wives realized what stuff they were

putting outside their face and some husbands knew what stuff they were putting inside, they'd die of shock! But, delighting in their respective bargains, they both enjoy the bliss of ignorance.

Those who have never studied the subject of modern smuggling, and who regard smuggling as they regard any other form of lawbreaking, cannot understand how the practice can persist in these days of alleged progress. A certain amount of smuggling they admit to be reasonable. In spite of our police and our prisons, we have not wiped out the thief, the housebreaker, the forger, the blackmailer, the murderer. But that smugglers should deprive the revenue of, and thereby cost the taxpayer, some dozen million pounds per annum is beyond all rhyme and reason. What, in the name of sanity, they demand, are the authorities doing about it?

Well, the Chief of the British Customs House receives a salary of 3000 pounds a year—one hundred-thousandth of the total sum he is responsible for collecting. The four other members of the Board of Commissioners receive salaries amounting to about another 8000 pounds, and these small basic items help to swell a total annual expense sheet of some *six millions!* That is to say, while the smuggler involves Great Britain in a defense expenditure of six millions, he still gets away with ten millions, thereby costing John Bull sixteen millions. It has been suggested that if another five millions were spent in his war against the smuggler, raising his army to the number of seventy thousand, he *might* be able to stamp out smuggling altogether. But, on the other hand, he might not. John Bull thinks he is spending quite enough.

The root of the problem lies in the root of human nature. The majority of us imagine, with our imperfect, material minds, that money is the most important thing in life, and that if we can devise any means of either making it or saving it, the ethical consideration must go to the wall. The sin to avoid is not the sin of commission, but the sin of being found out.

When smuggling decreases, as it did after the Napoleonic Wars, the decrease is not due to any change in the smuggler's moral or immoral sense. It is due to external circumstances which have rendered his job more difficult or less profitable—or both. Once upon a time, as we have seen, English folk were only interested in smuggling sheep. This was not because it was considered wrong to smuggle other articles, but only wool was worth the trouble. After the "owlers" had had their day, other commodities began to interest the illegal fraternity. Taxes and duties brought liquor and tea and tobacco into the limelight, till by the end of the eighteenth century the smugglers were in their prime and had an enormous choice to select from.

The end of the Napoleonic Wars permitted governments to "think inward" once more, and to devote some of their tired energy to troubles at home. The coast guards came into being, and by gradual degrees the smugglers grew fewer.

Free trade followed, and the spread of Liberal

ideals. Now the smuggler was not only up against
tightened authority, but his very incentive was being
squeezed dry! Confound Cobden! Blow Gladstone!
Everything was cheap now! What was a poor smuggler to do?

But then came Joseph Chamberlain. The smuggler
raised his nose. A breeze was beginning to blow again.
It bore sweet promise.

Free trade and Liberalism died hard. It needed a
war to smash them. The war smashed everything.
Wrongdoing thrives amid chaos, and also amid the
aftermath. It lurks among the scaffolding that is
erected for new buildings or to reinforce tottering
structures. The spirit of Joe Chamberlain smiled as
tariffs came into their own again, and more tariffs,
and yet more tariffs. In the wake of the tariffs came
the smugglers, and more smugglers, and yet more
smugglers, like the riffraff that follows an army.
Joseph Chamberlain did not want those, but hungry
wolves do not wait to be asked to a feast.

And then, as if some ironic god had decided to
recompense the smuggler for his dull period, there
came the Geddes ax. It fell, in 1923, upon the coast
guards, who had formed the nucleus of the ante-
Napoleonic drive. Three thousand picked men—men
of skill, courage and experience—were depleted by that
ax, an ax of good intentions but, in so far as the
customs were concerned, of bad results. The east
coast lay open again. Much, also, of other coasts. And
with countries struggling to adjust their economic
problems, restrictions rising, and politics in a tangle,

the world was as happy a playground for the smuggler as in the good old days of pistols and cutlasses.

No, it became a happier playground, for in the good old days contraband had the choice only of sea and land. Now was added the sky.

The complete history of smuggling cannot be written in our time. It has not been completed. It may transpire that, if nations persist in the example of "each for himself," the story of smuggling has only just begun! In any case, it is certain that the historian of the future will find more and more of his material above the clouds.

ENVOI

Here lies the Smuggler!
Never more
Will he lie watching
On the shore.
Here lie the lies
That he has told;
Here lies the contraband
He's sold.
Here lie his ankers
And his kegs.
Within this depth
Here lie his dregs.
Here lies the terror
He has spread—
With pain endured,
With pleasure read.
Here lies his courage
So ill spent;
Here lies his brain,
Misshapen, bent.
Here lies the myth
Of his belief
That to his folk
He brought relief.
He strode on dust;
His form now serves it.
Peace be his,
If he deserves it!

A SHORT GLOSSARY

OWLERS	*Wool-smugglers.*
CATERPILLARS	*Wool-smugglers.*
FLASKERS	*Liquor-smugglers.*
THE GENTLEMEN	*Any smugglers.*
DARKS	*Moonless nights.*
RUNNING GOODS	*Conveying contraband from the coast to its destination.*
CROP OF GOODS	*Contraband cargo.*
SINKING	*Concealing the crop under the sea.*
CREEPING	*Dragging the sea bottom for the crop.*
SWEEPING	*Dragging, with two boats.*
STINKIBUS	*Liquor rendered odoriferous by too long an immersion.*
SLINGING THE CASKS	*Fitting them with ropes for carrying.*
PORTERS	*Men who carried the casks.*
BATMEN	*Armed guards who protected the porters.*
SITTERS	*Officers in charge of preventive boats.*
HIDES	*Places for concealing contraband.*
TO VENTURE	*To invest in smuggling enterprises.*

DONKEYS	*One-legged rump-stools used by coast guards.*
GUARD	*Length of coast allotted to a coast guard.*
FLINK	*A smuggler's warning light.*

THE END

CPSIA information can be obtained
at www.ICGtesting.com
Printed in the USA
BVHW052243090223
658263BV00007B/159